THE PSYCHOLOGY OF TOURISM

Second Edition

Glenn F. Ross

James Cook University of North Queensland

Hospitality Press
MELBOURNE

To Carmel

Hospitality Press
38 Riddell Parade
PO Box 426
Elsternwick Victoria 3185
Australia
Telephone (03) 9528 5021 Fax (03) 9528 2645

Australian Studies in Tourism Series No 1
The Psychology of Tourism

First published 1994. Second edition 1998

National Library of Australia
Cataloguing-in-publication data:

Ross, Glenn F.
The psychology of tourism.
2nd ed.
    Bibliography.
    Includes index.
    ISBN 1 86250 480 6.
    1. Tourist trade – Psychological aspects. I. Title
    (Series: Australian studies in tourism; no. 1)
338.4791

Design and typesetting by John van Loon
Printed by Pearson Australia Demand Print Centre
Published by Hospitality Press Pty Ltd, Melbourne

Contents

Preface
to the second edition

The psychology of tourism has now become an important field of study. This book represents a contribution to the growing interface between tourism and psychology in both research and practice. While the book presents current findings from a variety of international perspectives, a focus in each chapter is on major applied psychological research as it now advances the boundaries of this tourism and psychology dialogue. This book is thus written as a contribution to the understanding of international tourism as well as the researcher's role in this enterprise.

SECTION 1

The Individual Tourist

1

Tourism and Psychology:
An Introduction

LEARNING OBJECTIVES

An understanding of:

- Various definitional approaches associated with tourism phenomena.
- Major models encapsulating the functioning of the tourism system.
- Historical forces shaping present day tourism.
- The utility of psychological understandings of tourism.
- A comparison between the study of leisure and the study of tourism.
- Tourism as a discipline.

Tourism is now a prominent industry in many parts of the world, and universities and tertiary education institutions are beginning to respond to the educational and research needs of this expanding industry. The study of tourism from the disciplinary perspective of psychology is an important element in this educational development. This book will outline some of the fundamental components of the study of tourism from a psychological standpoint. The book will do this along two dimensions: by way of an understanding of the behaviour of the individual tourist, and by way of an understanding of the social, the organisational and the community contexts of tourism.

Section One will examine major psychological topics such as motivation, personality, attitudes and the environment as they variously illuminate tourist behaviour. Section Two then explores conceptualisations of tourism in a number of societal contexts such as marketing, work organisations and human resource management, evaluation of tourism facilities and the social impacts of tourism on host communities. Throughout these chapters a number of themes will emerge. The material will address both conceptual and methodological issues. Practical applications as well as deficiencies in present knowledge will also be presented.

Finally, a variety of international studies will be presented, with each chapter concluding with findings from recent tourism research studies. This book will address the needs of those involved in tertiary education as well as those in the tourism/hospitality industry who believe that their organisation will profit from the application of ideas and findings from psychology to their present management and operational practices.

Conceptualisations of tourism

Burkart and Medlik (1981) assert that four major characteristics of tourists may be identified. They may be summarised thus:

1   They are people who undertake a journey to, and stay in, various destinations.
2   Their destinations are distinct from their normal place of residence and work, so that their activities are not the same as those of the resident and working populations of their destinations.
3   Their intention is to return within a few days or months, so the journey is of a temporary and short-term nature.
4   Their purpose for undertaking the journey is other than to take up permanent residence or employment remunerated from within the destinations.

They point out that generally the problem which arises in attempting to define tourism is not the distinctiveness of tourism but the difficulty of distinguishing tourism activities from other activities.

Cohen (1974) has outlined seven characteristics of tourism travel intended to delineate the tourist, by distinguishing the tourist from other travellers:

1   temporary, to distinguish it from the permanent travel undertaken by the tramp and nomad;
2   voluntary, to distinguish it from the forced travel of the exile and refugee;
3   round trip, to distinguish it from the one-way journey of the migrant;
4   relatively long, to distinguish it from the trip of the excursionist or tripper;
5   non-recurrent, to distinguish it from the recurrent trips of the holiday house owner;
6   non-instrumental, to distinguish it from the travel as a means to another end of the business traveller, travelling sales representative or pilgrim;

7   for novelty and change, to distinguish it from travel for other purposes such as study.

Another approach to this definitional problem can be recognised emerging in a series of definitions by bodies concerned with tourism data, starting with the Committee of Statistical Experts of the League of Nations in 1937 whose recommended definition of tourist was adopted by the Tourism Committee of the Organization for Economic Co-operation and Development. In 1968 the United Nations Statistical Commission and the International Union of Official Travel Organizations approved a similar definition proposed by the United Nations Conference on Travel and Tourism held in Rome in 1963, a definition which, with some minor changes, became that of the World Tourism Organisation:

> The term international visitor describes any person who travels to a country other than that in which he has his usual residence, the main purpose of whose visit is other than the exercise of an activity remunerated from within the country visited and who is staying for a period of one year or less. This definition covers two classes of visitors: international tourist and international excursionist which may be defined as follows:
>
> An international tourist is said to be a visitor in accordance with the above-mentioned definition staying at least one night but not more than one year in the country visited and whose main purpose of visit can be classified under:
> (a)   pleasure: holidays, culture, active sports, visits to friends and relatives, other pleasure purposes.
> (b)   professional: meeting, mission, business;
> (c)   other tourist purposes: studies, health, pilgrimage.
>
> An international excursionist is said to be a visitor in accordance with the above-mentioned definition who does not stay overnight in the country visited. (World Tourism Organization 1986: 240).

The Department for Economic and Social Information and Policy analysis of the United Nations (1992) has written that for statistical purposes, the term 'international visitor' describes 'any person who travels to a country other than that in which he/she has his/her usual residence but outside his/her usual environment for a period not exceeding 12 months and whose main purpose of visit is other than the exercise of an activity remunerated from within the country visited'.

International visitors are said to include:
(a)   Tourists, (overnight visitors): 'a visitor who stays at least one night in a collective or private accommodation in the country visited'; and
(b)   Same day visitors: 'a visitor who does not spend the night in collective or private accommodation in the country visited'.

Table 1.1 Morley's model of tourism

TOURIST	TOUR	OTHERS
Demand		
individual	prices	government policies
characteristics	fares	society & culture
income	promotion and	technology
age, sex, etc.	marketing	climate
motivations	attractions	political inter- and
		intra-national
		social trends
		economic trends
Supply		
stay duration	resources	infrastructure
activities	natural	roads
usage	built	sewerage
satisfaction	cultural	electricity
spending	tourism facilities	police
	& services	airports, etc.
	catering	communications
	transport	economy &
	reception	commerce
	accommodation	society
	entertainment	
	hospitality	
Impacts		
experience	income	environmental
knowledge	depreciation &	economic
pleasure	deterioration of	social
	resources	physical
	investment	

Source: Morley (1990)

The definition does not include immigrants, residents in a frontier zone, persons domiciled in one country or area and working in an adjoining country or area, members of the armed forces and diplomats and consular representatives when they travel from their country of origin to the country in which they are stationed and vice-versa. The definitions also exclude persons in transit who do not formally enter the country through passport control, such as air transit passengers who remain for a short period in a designated area of the air terminal or ship passengers who are not permitted to disembark. This would include passengers transferred directly between airports or other terminals. Other passengers in transit through a country are classified as visitors.

Models of tourism

Leiper's Model

Leiper (1990) has proposed a tourism systems model that can be used as a theoretical construct for general tourism analysis and discussion. This model contains both destination transit route and generators. This is shown in Figure 1.1 which depicts all five elements and their environments.

Leiper suggests that the model can be used for studies framed from the perspective of any element. The most common is from the perspective of a country or region in its role as a destination. Henshall and Robert's (1985) study of New Zealand as a destination in relation to several travel generating countries, incorporating a portfolio or products market matrix analysis, is said to be one example. Another insight is from the perspective of a country or region in its role as generator, with alternative destinations represented. This approach, it is argued, is useful for travel marketers, such as travel agencies and tour wholesalers.

The model, as a general systems framework, is also said to be useful for interdisciplinary studies of tourism. It is said to integrate, in a simple form, the typical components around which each discipline (Geography, Psychology, Economics, Management, etc.) can play its part in research or educational programs. The model is said not to be framed in a way that favours any particular discipline, leading to a biased or blinkered appreciation of the field. Rather, Leiper believes that it shows how their contributions can be organised to form a cohesive understanding of an otherwise complex subject.

Morley's model

Morley (1990) has also argued the need to consider concepts and characteristics of relevance in the context of a model of the tourism phenomenon. In

Figure 1.1 Leiper's Model of Tourism

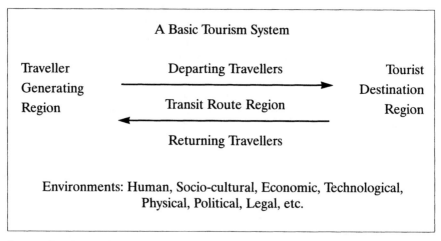

A Basic Tourism System

Traveller Generating Region   Departing Travellers   Tourist Destination Region

Transit Route Region

Returning Travellers

Environments: Human, Socio-cultural, Economic, Technological, Physical, Political, Legal, etc.

Source: Adapted from Leiper, 1990

this way complexities and relationships can be expressed more clearly in a scheme which has more of a dynamic and multi-dimensional capacity than any static definitional form. In proposing such a model (as in Table 1.1) Morley makes the point that two immediately necessary foundational elements of a model of tourism are the Tourist and the Tour, that is the person doing the travelling and staying and the destination, the organisation and the facilities that are the experience of the tourist. Because of the complexity, extent and impact of tourism there are said to be further involvements and impacts on 'Other' or parties such as governments, societies, economies and people indirectly involved. Thus three elements — Tourist, Tour and Other parties — are said to provide a basic characterisation of fundamental dimensions in a model of tourism (Morley 1990).

Morley further argues that the demand for tourism is a function of characteristics of the individual tourist such as their income, age, motivations and psychological make up, which will variously affect their propensity to travel for pleasure, their ability to travel and their choice of destinations. The demand is also said to be a function of characteristics and attributes of the tourism destinations, their attractions, prices and the effectiveness of the marketing of the destination. Government policies and actions are able to encourage or discourage tourism demand directly and with intent, and indirectly through factors which are important to tourists, such as security. Morley believes that social factors also can have an effect on demand, through the attitude of the local inhabitants towards the tourists and the interest generated by the local culture, for example. The demand then is said to affect the tourism supply. In terms of the tourists, Morley believes that the supply may be expressed in stay durations (for example, bed-nights), activities and resource usage of tourists (numbers of tourists, usage rates), satisfaction (ratings and return intentions) and spending (amounts of money). Facilities and services catering directly for tourists — hotels, restaurants, resorts, transport, etc. — are said to be the most immediately affected by tourism demand and therefore the most generally considered aspects of tourism seen as an industry with its economic impacts.

The relationships are said to be two-way, with demand to an extent determined by the supply of facilities and services. Although not necessarily provided for the benefit or use of tourists, many other facilities and services are used by tourists and those supplying to them, such as the infrastructure of the host country, communications facilities, and the general range of economic, commercial and social services available at the destination.

Morley also believes that the impacts of their experiences on individual tourists are fairly widely neglected, yet these can be of great importance, not just to the tourists themselves, but also in their impact on demand via the word of mouth spread of information, recommendations and repeat visits. The impacts of tourism on the tourism industry itself are said to be seen in investment and employment to meet the demand, and in the wear and tear on the tourism resources. Finally, there are seen to be wider impacts: the environmental, social and flow-on economic impacts. Each of the factors included in the Morley model is thus believed to be important to some aspect or parts of tourism, and could be taken as the focus for analysis in depth which, because of the inter-relationships between the factors, would necessarily include consideration of other factors in the model. The advantages of Morley's model over other models and conceptualisations of tourism are a consequence of its wider, more inclusive coverage of the areas and factors involved in the tourism phenomenon.

A brief history of tourism

Graburn and Jafari (1991) have pointed out that humans have always travelled. The early civilisations in the Middle East, Asia, and the Mediterranean have also left written records of their experiences. These records are said to reveal that as Greece, Rome and China expanded for trade and conquest, their upper classes often travelled for pleasure or diplomacy. Some commentators, such as Herodotus, wrote about travelling and sojourns, much as one might today. This long tradition of descriptive humanistic literature tells of the art and psychology of travel, as well as strangers and their manners, languages, religions, gift giving, lodging, and hospitality. Graburn and Jafari also make the point that the Age of Expansion and Exploration, by Arabs (800 AD on) and Europeans such as Marco Polo (1200 AD on), has left many travel accounts. Japanese travellers from the Edo period, such as the poet Bassho, wrote memoirs which still serve as guides for today's tourists in Japan. However, until the fifteenth century, they point out that most tourism was not for sightseeing, but to encounter important people and civilisations and to visit sacred places.

From the fifteenth century, European expansion was said to be enhanced by cartographic and sailing technologies, and the rise of the merchant classes, while travel documents multiplied through the newly invented printing press. According to these documents, Graburn and Jafari point out that from the mid-sixteenth century onwards, Northern Europeans regularly travelled to spas in their own countries, to centres of learning and to the ruins of the great classical civilisations of southern Europe. At first confined to nobles and diplomats, this circuit became commonplace. It became known as 'the tour' by the mid-1700s, and soon the term tourist was coined to describe participants in such pleasurable, educational journeys (Graburn and Jafari 1991). Taking two to three years at first, the tour gradually shortened as the number of tourists grew. The tourist (usually a young man) was said to be accompanied by a tutor, and many of them wrote of their travels in memoirs, travelogues, or guidebooks.

Graburn and Jafari point out that the records further show that in the nineteenth century, the Industrial Revolution and the social revolutions of imperialism, evangelism, and socialism brought vast social changes. They point out that Thomas Cook, an English Methodist reformer, used steam trains to take the urban poor to the countryside and to expositions and rallies. Seeing the commercial possibilities of mass tourism, he has been credited for inaugurating the modern tourist industry: travel agencies, reserved seats, booking hotels, accommodations classification, travellers' cheques, timetables, and comprehensive guidebooks. They believe that mass tourism at this point became an international enterprise.

In the decades following World War II tourism research has flourished, and Graburn and Jafari (1991) make the further point that in the 1960s the benefits of tourism were unquestioned. Research assumed that tourism was a labour-intensive growth industry beneficial to all. This notion, they assert, held that tourism brought in foreign exchange, employed more people, and that tourist expenditures had a large multiplier effect, stimulating the local economy and raising the standard of living. The massive tourist flows and projects that came into being were analysed and occasionally criticised. They point out that sociologists such as Knebel (1960) and Forster (1964) saw both the theoretical and applied importance of tourism research. They also mention that psychologists such as Farber (1954) and Reason (1964) examined the psychology of travel. Interest in tourism and heritage grew, they point out, and the parallel topic of tourism and ecology emerged. In Australia, psychologists such as P.L. Pearce have, over the last decade or so, investigated a wide range of tourism phenomena from the standpoint of a social psychologist.

Tourism and psychology

Pearce and Stringer (1991), commenting on the psychology-tourism interface have used a 'levels of analysis' approach, describing psychological enquiry as focusing variously on biological and physiological processes, cognitive and mental processes, individual differences, inter-individual behaviour, and cross-cultural or between-group behaviours. Thus, at one extreme, some studies of interest are said to be closely allied to medical and biological processes, while at the most general 'level', they argue that contemporary psychology is best conceived as the sum of these levels of study. Each of these levels of analysis is seen as having its own special methods, publication outlets, and scientific standing.

Despite this diversity of detail in contemporary psychology, there are some broad goals and methods which are said by them to unite the discipline. Most psychologists are said to pay attention to the behaviour and experience of individuals and seek to describe and, if possible, explain any observed patterns in that behaviour and experience.

In the methodological arena, there is said to be still a broad respect for experimental and empirical approaches to the topic of study. Additionally, new interpretive techniques and analyses (such as hermeneutic and social representational approaches) have a niche in the methodological panoply of contemporary psychology (Pearce and Stringer 1991). Pearce and Stringer conclude that there are few strongly opposed positions in the tourism or psychological literature, though the issue of whether tourists really learn much from their travels is one such debate. A broader conflict between psychology and other disciplines, they maintain, may also act as a galvanising force. They believe that in the absence of a broad psychological thrust in the discipline of tourism, geographers, sociologists, and leisure/recreation researchers are doing much work which at heart is psychological. They suggest that perhaps a territorial imperative will eventually be sufficient conflict to activate a much wider psychological inquiry.

Despite this lack of widespread interest among psychologists, the discipline of psychology has now commenced the development of a tradition of sound and useful research in the tourism domain. Mannell and Iso-Ahola (1987) have argued that conscious, immediate experiences, as well as the re-experience of these through recall from memory, are the important and primary outcomes of leisure and tourist behaviour. Recent research approaches to understanding consumer behaviour, even in the non-leisure and non-tourism areas have, they argue, focused increasingly on the more symbolic, emotive, and aesthetic side of behaviour.

Studying leisure and tourist experiential phenomena

Mannell and Iso-Ahola (1987) make the point that leisure theorists and researchers have given much more theoretical and empirical consideration to the nature of leisure experiences and states than tourism scholars have to the phenomenology of tourism. They believe that examination of the actual psychological research reported on leisure as experience suggests that three approaches can be distinguished. These are generally called definitional, post-hoc satisfaction, and immediate conscious experience approaches. Mannell and Iso-Ahola make the point that the three approaches are similar in that leisure is most profitably understood from the subjective perspective of the participant, yet they differ in how they treat or conceptualise this subjectivity. The definitional approach here advanced by Mannell and Iso-Ahola focuses on the perceived situational determinants leading to the perception of leisure, without explicitly identifying the typography of the experience itself. The post-hoc satisfaction approach has focused on the perceived motivations, outcomes, and satisfactions associated with the experience. The immediate conscious experience approach is said to be committed to the value of monitoring the actual, on-site, real-time nature of the experience itself (Mannell and Iso-Ahola, 1987).

They argue that from the definitional standpoint much is known about the factors that influence people's perceptions and labelling of their activities and the resulting experiences as leisure or non-leisure. Leisure researchers, it is said, have been able not only to identify the major ingredients of subjective definitions of leisure (sense of freedom, intrinsic motivation, enjoyment, relaxation) but also some of the conditions which influence the importance of these factors. On the other hand, Mannell and Iso-Ahola point out that little research has been done on tourism from the definitional perspective. They point out that although theorists have suggested that the search for the ultimate tourist experience is a quest (for example, authenticity, centre, meaning, and values), but little theory or research has been reported which identifies the basic dimensions of defining criteria of authentic meaningful tourism episodes. Mannell and Iso-Ahola pose questions such as: What factors lead people to describe an activity or a set of activities as authentic tourism or touristic experiences? Are these personal definitions similar to those of tourist operators or researchers? Are authentic touristic experiences leisure experiences? Are there other meaningful dimensions by which tourists label and define their experiences? Such questions would seem useful to explore within the Australian tourism context.

In regard to the post-hoc satisfaction approach, Mannell and Iso-Ahola say that both leisure and tourist researchers have followed the same route. In the factor-analytic studies, subjects have been presented with a large number of reasons and then asked to rate the importance of each reason for their leisure or tourist participation. They argue that these ratings, however, have been done as general statements rather than in relation to specific leisure/ touristic experiences. The same strategy, it is said, has been used in the case of satisfaction measures. As a result, many important research questions, they believe, remain unanswered. A new theoretical framework has recently been developed by these researchers to explain both leisure and tourism motivation. According to this two-dimension theory, two motivational forces simultaneously influence the individual's leisure or tourist behaviour. Psychological benefits of leisure travel experiences are said to emanate from the interplay of two forces: escaping of routine and stressful environments and seeking recreational opportunities for certain intrinsic rewards. A recent trend towards more frequent, but shorter vacations suggests to Mannell and Iso-Ahola that the escape dimension is a more important motivational force than the seeking dimension for tourism. At the same time, research is said to indicate people escape both over- and under-stimulating life situations through vacations in efforts to achieve and maintain their optimal level of arousal. If they escape over-stimulation, they are said to participate in fewer leisure activities during a vacation and the seeking of intrinsic rewards becomes less important for them than for those who escape under-stimulation. It is concluded by Mannell and Iso-Ahola that while this basic motivational mechanism is the same for tourism and other leisure behaviours, tourism is said more likely to be triggered by the escape motive because of the travel industry's constant promotion of the need to escape over- or under-stimulating everyday environments.

In respect of immediate conscious experience, they point out that leisure research has also given this issue greater attention than has tourism research. According to this approach, the anatomy of the experience, its intensity, duration, memorability, and meaning ought to be subjected to scientific analysis. Researchers, they point out, have discovered that flow is the core of leisure experience, and claim to have identified the central elements of flow experiences (e.g. centring of attention and becoming totally involved in the activity at hand). While a variety of methods has been used to uncover the regularities in how people experience the stream of consciousness, the Experiential

Sampling Method is said by Mannell and Iso-Ahola to be the reason for the recent series of studies focusing on the on-site content of leisure experience. They call for respondents to carry electronic pagers with them during the course of their daily activity, and upon random signalling, fill out a brief questionnaire. This beeper methodology is said to have produced many informative and insightful studies on various aspects of leisure experience, but unfortunately has not been applied to analysing tourist experience. They also point out that the use of the diary method has been rare. This leaves the information about the relationship between leisure experience and tourist experience inconclusive in their view. In spite of some intuitively obvious similarities between the two, at present, it is said not possible to conclude when and under what conditions tourist experience becomes leisure experience (Mannell and Iso-Ahola 1987).

The Discipline of Tourism

Tribe (1997) has examined the notion of tourism as a separate discipline, using conceptual tools taken from the philosophy of knowledge and the sociology of knowledge. Tribe concludes that tourism does not yet possess an overarching paradigm or unifying theory, and has thus far not reached disciplinary status. Further, he suggests that tourism may be best understood as comprising two distinct fields: approaches which are basically focused in the world of thought, and approaches which are focused in the world of practice. Tribe warns that the fundamental values held by those operating from the different approaches to tourism may vary considerably. He suggests that varying ideologies may make communication between these two fields problematic. He also suggests that different groups may speak a different technical language and therefore may not share an entirely common communication process. Problems may be framed differently by the respective groups and this may occasion dispute as to what factors are appropriate to enter the frame.

It is also suggested that the academic world may have some tendency to undervalue the type of knowledge generated by the world of practice. Tribe makes the point that more collaborating projects between the tourism industry and higher education may reduce this industry/academy dysfunction. Tribe further suggests that the quest for tourism to be generally recognised as a discipline ought to be abandoned. Such a quest as this, he believes, is likely to involve the exclusion of some valuable parts of tourism studies as the price to be paid for conceptual coherence and logical consistency. Finally, Tribe sees no great problem for tourism to be regarded as being at a pre-paradigmatic phase in its development. This characteristic is regarded more as a strength, something of great value.

Summary

This chapter has introduced the reader to a number of basic topics which may be regarded as starting points in the study of tourism from a psychological standpoint. Conceptual and definitional issues are examined as are psychological contexts and historical overviews. The following chapters will present the tourism/psychology interface from both a theoretical and applied perspective, developing the theme that tourism is most comprehensively understood by taking regard of both individual tourist behaviour and the context in which it occurs.

CHAPTER 1 DISCUSSION TOPICS

How do tourists differ from other types of travellers?

Tourist experiences can be major, and sometimes neglected. Describe these impacts in areas such as the tourist, tour and others.

Outline the various levels at which it is possible to study the psychology of tourism.

Explore some of the domains in which it is claimed that leisure theorists are somewhat more advanced than are tourism theorists.

Outline Tribe's view of tourism as a discipline.

2

Motivation and the Tourist

LEARNING OBJECTIVES

An understanding of:

- The complexities of the relationships between work and leisure.
- The basic motivation of behaviour, both in a general sense and in the tourism context.
- The motivation for travel and non-travel from a social welfare perspective.
- Travel careers.
- Motivation and expectations.

This chapter will address issues associated with the topic of motivation and tourist behaviour. It will do so by first examining the relationship and contrast between work life and tourism so as to examine issues such as how work affects tourist behaviour, the boundaries between work behaviour and tourism, and also the various conceptualisations offered to explain the relationship between the two. The chapter will also provide an understanding of motivation within the context of general psychology, and will then proceed to a coverage of the motivations of tourist behaviour from various theoretical perspectives as well as applied studies. The chapter will then provide an examination of the converse of tourism motivation: why it is that some do not take on the role of tourist. The chapter will conclude with a coverage of studies involving the application of motivational theory to tourist behaviour.

The tourism/work relationship

The investigation of the tourism/work dichotomy has received relatively little research attention by scholars from the social sciences. An associated subject, the work/leisure relationship has received somewhat more attention by social and behavioural scientists. This chapter will examine the tourism/work relationship as it sheds light on the motivation of tourists, and will do so by way of an application of a number of leisure concepts to the domain of tourist behaviour.

There have been a number of explanations offered to comprehend the relationships between leisure and work that may be relevant to the tourism/work relationship (see Mitchell, Dowling, Kabanoff and Larson 1988; Kabanoff and O'Brien 1986). The most prominent of these is generally referred to as the 'spillover' effect. Here it is assumed that the nature of a person's work directly influences the person in choosing tourist activities in one of two ways:

1   Positive spillover, where a work characteristic desirable to the worker is found in chosen leisure.
2   Negative spillover, where an undesirable aspect of work spills over into leisure activities.

The spillover theory assumes, as a basic tenet, that attitudes and habits acquired during work are so deeply ingrained that they are inevitably carried over into chosen tourist behaviour. Thus Mitchell *et al.* point out that an individual whose work demands planning and precision may well choose holidays and make detailed holiday arrangements which leave little or nothing to chance.

A second major theoretical postulate which may explain work/tourism relationships is that known as the compensatory hypothesis. This theory generally holds that deprivations experienced at work are made up or compensated for, in non-work settings. Kabanoff and O'Brien point out that the compensatory theory is said to have two possible outcomes:

1   Supplemental or positive compensation — in which desirable experiences, behaviours, psychological states (like autonomy, status, self-fulfilment) that are absent or in short supply in the work setting, are pursued in a leisure context, and
2   Reactive or negative compensation — undesirable work experiences are redressed in a non-work or leisure setting (like letting off steam in response to job tension, or resting from physically fatiguing work).

Kabanoff and O'Brien argue that another important, but perhaps less obvious, theoretical point is the distinction between free time or leisure and non-free, non-work time. One person might see the time he/she has to spend with his/her family limiting his/her leisure time, while another might view the time he/she chooses to be with family as intrinsically rewarding leisure time. They believe that it thus is instructive to explore people's perceptions as to whether or not they see themselves as having a choice or not in their non-work activities, and how this affects their perceptions of these activities as leisure.

Banner and Himmelfarb (1985) argue that an approach such as phenomenology may be a useful concept in this context. This emphasises the actors' perceptions (their definitions of the situation), and also inevitably recognises the interpretative process whereby actors handle and modify their meanings. They point out that some authors have noted that meanings are not fixed and immutable. They vary from situation to situation. What is work one day may be tourist behaviour another. The extent to which these definitions are situational, or trans-situational, is said to be as much an empirical question as a theoretical one. In addition to viewing voluntarism as a crucial variable in work and tourism, they argue that it is useful also to examine the type of reward sought (or received) in performing an activity.

Much attention in the worker motivation literature has been paid to the distinction between intrinsic and extrinsic rewards. If a person is seen doing an activity for some goal independent of the activity (e.g. higher pay, promotion, status) that person is said to be extrinsically motivated. Intrinsic motivation, on the other hand, they point out, refers to the pleasure or value associated with the activity itself.

Intrinsic motivation they suggest may be broken down into two categories:

1   Intrinsic valence associated with task behaviour, and
2   Intrinsic valence associated with task accomplishment.

Banner and Himmelfarb (1985) say that there is significant empirical support for the notion that task accomplishment and task behaviour can be rewarding to an individual, independent of any externally mediated rewards. These findings they have applied to the tourism/work relationship. Table 2.1 contains a diagram to aid in the understanding of this model, adapted by the present author for tourism.

Cell 1 encompasses those individuals who work at jobs/activities because they are intrinsically interesting, yet also necessary. This type of work may be described as interesting and perceived to be necessary for some psychological reason. In contrast, Cell 2 is more the standard conceptualisation of work for many people. It is work that is perceived to be necessary in order to earn a living and may evince few if any positive psychological perceptions. Thus it is done only for the money. Cell 3 maybe described as 'pure tourism' — it summarises those who choose tourism activities/destinations/outcomes because of their intrinsic value and potential enjoyment. Cell 4 encompasses those non-work activities that fall somewhere between voluntary tourism and work. This could cover a range of non-work non-tourism activities such as family and civic

Table 2.1 Tourism/work typology adapted from the leisure/work typology

Type of Reward	Type of Voluntarism	
	Compulsory	Voluntary
Intrinsic	Fun Work (Cell 1)	Tourism (Cell 3)
Extrinsic	Work (Cell 2)	Obligatory Tourism (Cell 4)

Adapted from Banner and Himmelfarb, 1985.

obligations wherein an individual visits distant family or discharges social/civic obligations in another place. This cell would also cover tourism undertaken for status reasons — i.e. a visit to a particular destination or engaging in a tourist activity because it is fashionable and perceived to be able to advance a person socially or in the eyes of others.

One might then, as Banner and Himmelfarb (1985) have done for leisure, view the tourism/work distinction, not as a dichotomy, but, rather, as two typologies at opposite ends of a continuum. At the tourist end, there are those activities which people see as matters of personal choice; at the work end, we have those activities people view as a matter of compulsion. This view allows the consideration of different conceptions of work as well as tourism. It is clear that work means something different to one who feels he/she does not have to work. For him/her, the tourism/work distinction may be blurred. His/her work would fall towards the leisure end of the continuum. There is also the person who finds his/her greatest fun in work because he/she is doing precisely what he/she chooses. If one also finds no direct or simple relationship between work and tourism for some people, perhaps the distinction is a meaningless one for them.

General theories of motivation

This section will examine major motivational theories within modern psychology that have been suggested as having considerable potential for the understanding of tourist motivation.

Maslow's needs hierarchy

Maslow's needs hierarchy is one of the best-known theories of motivation. It is cited in most, if not all undergraduate psychology texts; it has been influential in industrial and organisational psychology as a theory of work motivation and is commonly quoted in other applied areas, such as counselling, marketing and tourism. Briefly, Maslow suggested that human needs as motivators form a hierarchy. He initially proposed (Maslow 1943) a five-level hierarchy, comprising physiological, safety, love, esteem and self-actualisation needs (see Table 2.2). He later added to these two other sets of needs, the need to know and understand, and aesthetic needs (Maslow 1954), but it is not entirely clear how these needs were to fit into the original hierarchy. Maslow argued that if none of the needs in the hierarchy was satisfied, then the lowest needs, the physiological ones, would dominate behaviour. If these were satisfied, however, they would no longer motivate, and the individual would be motivated by the next level in the hierarchy, the safety needs. Once these were satisfied, the individual would move up to the next level, continuing to work up the hierarchy as the needs at each level were satisfied.

Table 2.2 Basic components of Maslow's needs hierarchy

Physiological Needs	Hunger, thirst, sex, sleep, air, etc.
Safety Needs	Freedom from threat or danger; a secure, orderly and predictable environment.
Love Needs	Feelings of belonging, affectionate relationships, friendship, group membership.
Esteem Needs	Self-respect, achievement, self-confidence, reputation, recognition, prestige.
Need for Self-actualisation	Self-fulfilment, realising one's potential.

Source: Adapted from Maslow, 1943.

Two general points may be made about Malsow's theory of motivation:

1   His theory was originally constructed in the context of areas such as clinical psychology. The application, however, is now starting to occur within the Psychology of Tourism field.

2   The needs hierarchy has received some criticisms. These criticisms will be outlined in Chapter 7 when the topic of work motivation is covered. Notwithstanding such criticisms, Maslow's theory has received some support within tourism research (e.g. Pearce 1982b, Ross 1992b). The case study at the conclusion of this chapter is a contribution to this process.

Murray's classification of human needs

Another motivation theory from mainstream psychology which may offer explanatory promise within the Psychology of Tourism domain is Murray's needs theory. However, Murray's classification does not adapt as readily as Maslow's needs hierarchy to easy presentation to non-psychologists. It would seem the case that Murray's theory of human needs appears not to be as easy to comprehend as is Maslow's. The point is sometimes made that unlike Maslow, Murray believed that needs will change independently. Therefore knowing the strength of one need will not necessarily explain anything about the strength of others. Some commentators have thus suggested that perhaps for this reason, Murray's work on human needs never became as popular as Maslow's did. Nevertheless, there has been much research into specific needs, particularly the needs for achievement, affiliation, autonomy and power. A number of basic needs are given in Table 2.3, in which it can be seen that Murray's needs theory offer considerable scope for the exploration of needs and travel destination decisions. As yet relatively little research has been completed in this area, and thus considerable potential for future motivational research here remains. A study of Murray's needs within the tourism/work context will be presented in Section 2.

Table 2.3 A Selection of Murray's Classification of Human Needs which may be applicable to tourist behaviour

Achievement	To feel that something difficult has been accomplished.
Dominance	To control other people. To organise the behaviour of a group.
Autonomy	To value and strive for a sense of independence.
Affiliation	To mingle with and enjoy the company of others.
Play	To relax, amuse oneself, seek diversion and entertainment. To 'have fun', to play games. To laugh, joke and be merry. To avoid serious tension.
Cognisance	To explore. To ask questions. To satisfy curiosity. To look, listen, inspect. To read and seek knowledge.

Tourist motivation: quasi-psychological theories

The commentators Burkart and Medlik (1981) appear to have relatively little to say about fundamental processes of motivation. They basically quote Gray's (1970), two central motivations:

Wanderlust — the desire to exchange the known for the unknown, to leave things familiar and to go and see different places, people, and cultures or relics of the past in places famous for their historical monuments and associations or for their current fashions and contributions to society.

Sunlust — a type of travel which depends on the existence else where of better amenities for a specific purpose than are available in the domicile; it is prominent with particular activities such as sports and literally the search for the sun. (p. 57).

Crompton (1979b) has articulated nine motives so as to explain tourism motivation — seven classified as socio-psychological or push motives and two classified as cultural or pull motives. The motives are: Escape from a perceived mundane environment, Exploration and evaluation of self, Relaxation, Prestige, Regression, Enhancement of kinship relationships, Facilitation of social interaction, Novelty and Education.

Mayo and Jarvis (1981) have cited work by McIntosh (1977) who suggested that travel motivations could be divided into four categories:

- Physical Motivators: physical rest, sports participation, beach recreation, relaxing entertainment, and health considerations.
- Cultural Motivators: the desire for knowledge of other countries — their music, art, folklore, dances, paintings, and religion.
- Interpersonal Motivators: the desire to meet new people; to visit friends or relatives; to escape from routine, family, or neighbours; or to make new friendships.
- Status and Prestige Motivators: the desire for recognition, attention, appreciation and a good reputation. (p. 148)

Motivation and non-travellers

Most studies of motivation and tourism, for obvious and necessary reasons, concentrate on people who actually travel. Rarely, if ever, do researchers seek to study motivation by looking at the converse of this topic: non-travellers. Yet a study of non-travellers may also shed some light on tourist motivation. This section will consider such a topic, and focus on individuals who seldom or never assume the tourist role. In particular it will provide a brief examination of what characterises the social situation of this group of people, the reasons that non-travellers give for not participating in tourism activities, and the ways in which they interpret their situations.

In discussing causal forces and leisure patterns within society, Settle, Alreck and Belch (1978) have made the point that there has been a general development during recent decades in which classic social background variables seem to have become less important as explanatory and motivation factors. Neither social class nor occupational prestige is said to constitute an effective indicator of leisure preferences. A possible explanation offered here is that the highly dynamic social structure of countries such as the United States has gradually diminished the major differences between various social strata. They believe that if this is the case, it parallels the process of equalisation observed in many countries now concerning the tendency of different social groups to take holiday trips.

Social welfare and travel motivation

Haukeland (1990) has made the point that in Scandinavian countries, the concept of social tourism means that everybody, regardless of economic or social situation, should have the opportunity to go on vacation. Holiday travel is thus viewed like any other human right whose social loss should be compensated by the welfare state. Haukeland points out that the fact that farmers in Norway have been guaranteed a three-week holiday during the summer period (since the mid-1970s, as a relief system financed by the state) illustrates that this kind of view has penetrated the political systems. Greater equality in this domain of life quality has become regarded as a worthwhile ideal. Norms, it is said, have been established to remove physical obstacles for disabled persons in hotels and other areas of life. However, more direct political measures, whereby socially deprived groups are introduced to tourism, have not yet been introduced. He points out that such attempts have until now been the domain of private initiative through charitable organisations and special interest groups.

Haukeland argues that this normative link between social welfare and vacationing in fact implies that opportunities to go on holiday should be treated as an important indicator of social well-being. In this context, the number of people who are obliged to stay at home, and the economic and social factors involved, should, it is argued, be a major area for further research. In addition to this ideological connection, the causal relationship between social welfare and holiday opportunities can also be studied. Haukeland argues that if one's personal or household living conditions are unsatisfactory, these will, in most cases, restrict the quantity and quality of choice opportunities available to that individual. Similarly, the boundaries surrounding possible alternatives open to any individual often extend into the field of holiday travel. In analysing the phenomenon of staying at home, Haukeland (1990) believes it is useful to dichotomise these two dimensions. Under this social-right perspective, there is a fundamental difference between those persons who are obliged to stay at home and those who actually have the opportunity to take a vacation, but still prefer to remain at home for one reason or another. In the latter case, the main question for Haukeland is whether or not a person's decision to forego travel can be described as an effect of an unsatisfactory social situation.

The two dichotomies are combined in a four-component model. Haukeland's matrix yields a typology of different non-travelling characteristics:

- Type A represents persons who are not confronted with any obstacles to going on vacation. Their general social situation is also unproblematic. Nevertheless, these individuals prefer to stay at home in order to maximise their well-being.
- Type B is somewhat more complex. Here the social living conditions are satisfactory. However, other constraints prevent these individuals from taking holiday trips. Such obstacles are either temporary or permanent.
- Type C encompasses constrained non-travellers who are placed in an unsatisfactory social situation. The problem here might be of a welfare type (lack of economic means, health resources, personal freedom, etc.) or more complex in nature. Non-travel under such circumstances reflects social welfare problems, and the additional deprivation. In certain cases non-travel can reinforce social problems.
- Type D represents unconstrained non-travel with unsatisfactory living conditions which is of logical possibility. Empirically, it probably occurs rarely and is also of more peripheral interest for the topic at hand.

These four typologies, he argues, can be quite useful in conceptualising non-travelling characteristics within a social welfare perspective. However, Haukeland points out that the relationship between social welfare and travelling opportunities is by no means exhausted by this model. Constrained non-travelling embraces more (i.e. Type B) than simply the effect of unsatisfactory social living conditions (i.e. Type A). On the other hand, the fact that a problematic social situation does not necessarily lead to the foregoing of holiday travel is said not to be reflected in the typology, since this paradigm only relates to varieties of non-travelling. In spite of social problems, resources might be available to realise the holiday trip. Haukeland finally makes the point that it should, therefore, be noted that an unsatisfactory social situation is neither a necessary nor a sufficient condition explaining the phenomenon of non-travel.

Travel careers

Pearce and Caltabiano (1983) argue that research concerning travel motiva-tion has frequently assumed that tourists are both able and willing to articu-late their travel needs. Their study adopts a different point of view by arguing that indirect inferences about travel motivation from tourists' actual experi-ences may provide access to a further layer of insight. Using nearly 400 trav-el episodes and employing a five-fold classification of travel motivation based on Maslow's analysis of needs, Pearce and Caltabiano report that a wide range of travel experiences were accommodated successfully in this coding scheme. Results indicated that positive and negative tourist experiences were not the inverse of one another but highlighted different need structures. Overall they have demonstrated that there is a motivational career in travel, with more experienced travellers reporting experiences containing more higher-order needs. Female travellers also recorded slightly more self-actualisation needs than men. They have argued that the tourist motivational literature could be well-served by this kind of indirect motivational coding scheme. Figure 2.1 contains Pearce and Caltabiano's career model.

Figure 2.1 Suggested steps in tourists' travel careers

[Self-actualisation
needs]   **Self-actualisation**

      (Cultural)
      (Historical)
[Self-esteem **Self-development** (Environmental)
needs]   (Authenticity)

    Family, intimate relationships

Seeking   [Love and belong-
relationships   ingness needs]

Prestige   **Novelty** **Novelty** [Security or its
    (place) (activities) inverse arousal-
      related needs]

Relaxation **Physiological** **Activities**

(e.g. sleep, (food, drink, (sport, [physiolological
get away) casual sex) recreation) needs]

The steps in a tourist's travel career are organised as a part of an ascending or hierarchically inclusive adaptation of Maslow's five levels of motivation. The corresponding Maslow levels are indicated in square brackets.

Source: Pearce (1988)

They have suggested that several small but valuable advances in motivation research concerning tourists have emerged from this study. Firstly, they report that it has proved to be practical and possible to code tourist experiences in a five-fold Maslow-based category scheme of motivation from tourists' reported social episodes. Additionally, the results suggested that the motivations realised in positive experiences were quite unlike those from tourists threatened by negative experiences. In positive experiences, tourists were not concerned with safety and self-esteem but found rewards in the fulfilment of physiological, love and belongingness and self-actualising needs. The coding of the negative experiences was concerned with the thwarting of self-actualising experiences. They concluded that the negative experiences also fit neatly into Maslow's notion of a hierarchy of needs, with lower-order needs dominating travellers' concerns in stressful circumstances.

A second aim of their study was to explore the relationships between previous motivational profiles and that obtained by their methodology. They admit that direct comparisons are only meaningful with exactly the same corpus of respondents. However, they believe that the current method emphasised the existence of a high proportion of love and belongingness in all travellers and a proportion of self-actualisation needs in experienced travellers. Their study also generated important information on the safety needs of tourists and their concern to avoid losses of self-esteem. These latter concerns regarding self-esteem are expressed infrequently in the direct self-report travel motivation literature. They argue that it is desirable to conduct further studies directly comparing the inferred motivation technique offered here and the self-report approaches. They suggest from the above points that the inferred motivation technique can add fresh perspectives to this realm of tourist research.

They also found that the notion that tourists may be thought of as having a motivational career in travel was also sustained by their data. In particular, the two experienced traveller groups (those who had visited either more than three or more than 10 countries) were shown to be more concerned with higher-order needs (notably love and belongingness and self-actualisation) than were less experienced travellers. For the negative motivations, the results were found to be less clear-cut, but the two groups of experienced travellers were more concerned with threats to their self-esteem and self-actualisation goals (higher-order needs) than their less experienced counterparts. They report that both groups of experienced travellers were proportionally more concerned with safety considerations, perhaps because they fully appreciated, through their own contacts, some of the dangers of extensive travel.

The section of their results dealing with sex differences and positive needs contained the finding that female travellers compared to males were somewhat more concerned with self-actualisation needs. It appeared that males, not females, were those who were proportionately more concerned with love and belongingness needs. Pearce and Caltabiano suggest that this finding, though perhaps initially counter-intuitive, may reflect less on traditional sex roles and areas of female concern with relationships than on the special self-actualising role travel can play in the lives of women. In summary, such findings provide starting points for a range of further research projects. The results of this study by Pearce and Caltabiano represent a major contribution to tourism motivation research which has been conducted by psychology researchers.

Motivation and expectation formation

Gnoth (1997) has adumbrated a tourist motivation process which illustrates the central role played by the formation of expectations. The bases of motivations are said to be felt needs which, when combined with situational characteristics and value structures, influence tourists' perception of an object. The expectations and attitudes held towards any tourism entity are said to be closely related to the tourists' felt needs and value systems. These expectations, according to Gnoth, are emotion-dominant and possess the characteristics of self-directed drives. Thus a touristic object may be targeted because of its perceived promise to satisfy psychological needs and values. Gnoth points out that objects targeted by such motivational processes can vary widely and be subject to substitution. It is suggested that a tourist's need for and value of excitement may be met by a range of activities, including reading a thrilling novel through to bungee jumping.

It is also suggested by Gnoth that there are outer-directed values which target very specific objects. Such motivational forces are cognition-dominant and their objects are not amenable to substitution in the way that inner-directed values are. Moreover, Gnoth points out that inner-directed value processes can be expected to demonstrate a reduced drive once satisfied, while outer-directed value processes do not. Indeed such processes, it is argued, actually strengthen their role in the tourist's cognitive functions. Gnoth suggests that this motivation formulation, bringing together notions such as motives and values, facilitates a clearer understanding of cultural, social and situational factors as they may indicate tourist motivational processes. Values and attitudes which relate to preferences and choices associated with destinations, activities, transport and other tourism-related phenomena are said to be distinguished according to their cognition versus emotion import. Gnoth further holds that measurement of these constructs may be pursued by way of standard attitude-measurement techniques for the outer-directed conservatively based values. However, for the inner-directed drives he suggests a very different approach, one less likely to be linked to the measurement of objects of experience. Here the focus is on an understanding of subjective but nonetheless important notions such as an understanding of process, flow, and perception of internal states.

Summary

This chapter has examined the psychological domain of motivation as it may be applied to tourism behaviour. It took as its starting point an examination of some of the conceptualisations of the tourism/work interface so as to delineate the parameters of tourism motivation. The chapter has also provided a coverage of two major psychological theories of motivation along with a coverage of motivational studies within the tourism context. The chapter has then reviewed the opposite to tourism motivation: those who for various reasons do not travel. Finally, the chapter considers travel and tourism motivation.

CHAPTER 2   DISCUSSION TOPICS

Outline Murray's classification of human needs, and apply them to tourist behaviour.

Discuss the psychological processes which have been advanced to explain the work/tourism association.

How are Physical, Cultural, Interpersonal, and Status and Prestige motivators defined?

Describe briefly some of the causal forces said to be associated with leisure preference changes in western society.

How has a major motivational construct been applied to the notion of travel career?

3

Personality and the Tourist

LEARNING OBJECTIVES

An understanding of:

- The complexity of personality constructs together with their utility in understanding tourist behaviour.
- The basic components of the allocentric/psychocentric model of personality as applied to tourist behaviour.
- The applications of personality constructs to tourism.
- A justification for ethical behaviour in the tourism context.
- Group holiday decision-making.

Personality is perhaps one of the best known topics within the discipline of psychology. This chapter will commence with an examination of the notion of personality from the domain of mainstream psychology, and then provide a coverage of one of the most widely known and explored applications of personality conceptualisations to tourism, that of Plog's allocentric/psychocentric typology of tourist behaviour. The chapter will further consider criticisms and refinements of Plog's model. It will then examine a study which has explored personality measures in the comprehension of tourist behaviour. The chapter will conclude with an exploration of tourism ethics and also group holiday decision-making.

Personality — the psychological construct

Schultz (1981) has pointed out that there are at least nine theories of personality: psychoanalytic, neopsychoanalytic, interpersonal, trait, developmental, humanistic, cognitive, behaviouristic, and limited-domain. In some cases, these viewpoints represent major forces active throughout psychology, not just in the area of personality. He believes that, although this organisation of theories allows for a meaningful presentation of individual systems of personality, it will not supply a single answer to the question 'What is personality?' There is no neat or simple answer — at least not yet in psychology. The complexity of the subject matter is said to be evident in the diversity of the attempts to come to grips with it. As to which, if any, of these theories or approaches is the best or ultimate answer, who is to say? For Schultz, only those persons already committed, intellectually and emotionally, to one position, and thus perhaps no longer able to take an objective view, can answer that question with certainty.

He makes the point that this is not to suggest that one of these theories may turn out to be correct and all the others wrong. The study of personality would not appear as simple as that. That theories are said to conflict on occasions with one another does not necessarily indicate that they are misguided and destined to fall into disrepute. Schultz believes that any one theory may be partly correct or all of them may be partly correct, and the final answer may involve the combination of part-truths into yet another higher-order theory. Thus, although it may eventually transpire that none of the present theories will suffice as the complete explanation, for now they represent the level of development of that part of psychology attempting to understand the human personality.

The utility of personality

Schultz makes the point that the lack of agreement among theorists does not necessarily imply that the various theories are not useful. Psychologists are said to not agree on a single definition of intelligence, but that has not prevented them from using the concept of intelligence in a variety of useful ways to understand and predict human behaviour. Each of the personality theories mentioned above offers interesting and useful insights into human nature — conclusions based, for the most part, on years of patient probing, questioning, and listening to what people have to say, or observing their behaviour under the rigorous conditions of the experimental laboratory. These theories are said to be the work of highly perceptive and intelligent individuals, each of whom has looked closely at humankind through the uniquely ground lens of his or her theoretical viewpoint.

All of the theorists, it is said, have some important, impressive, and provocative statements to make about the nature of human beings. If they do not always agree, it is said, to be useful to look to three factors to explain the dissension: (1) the complexity of the subject matter, (2) the differing historical and personal contexts in which each theory was formulated, and (3) the fact that psychology is such a young discipline, a recent entry in the catalogue of sciences. Indeed, the very facts of its newness and complexity make personality for Schultz an intriguing subject for study. It is not a closed or finished subject in which one learns the rules and definitions and then moves on to something else. On the contrary, the study of personality is still evolving, and for those who like the challenge and excitement of applying concepts not yet fully mapped, there could be no more appropriate or useful study than personality as it illuminates tourist behaviour.

The definition of personality

Schultz believes that the lack of agreement about the nature of personality and which approach is most effective to study it is reflected by an equal amount of disagreement with regard to the word itself. In his classic study of personality, Allport (1937) discussed some 50 definitions of personality. Rather than describing these and the many definitions offered since his work, it would seem more useful to relate personality to an everyday usage of the term. It is a word that people all use at some time, however, loosely or inaccurately, and that we all feel we know the meaning of.

Personality, it is said, may also refer to enduring characteristics. Schultz argues that theorists assume a degree of stability and predictability in a person's personality. Personality, therefore, is not rigid and unchanging. It is also held by Schultz that personality is unique to each of us. While we recognise similarities among people, we sense that individuals possess special properties or combinations of properties that distinguish them from one another. Thus, in everyday life, we tend to think of personality as an enduring and unique cluster of characteristics. But this is not a definition on which all psychologists would agree. To achieve any degree of precision in defining the concept, it is important for Schultz to understand what each theorist means by his or her own use of the term. Each theorist is said to offer a unique version — a personal insight of the nature of personality — and that view thus becomes a definition of the term. Thus tourism researchers are offered a veritable banquet in regard to dimensions and conceptualisations which might be profitably explored in the touristic domain.

Psychographics and tourism

This section will provide a coverage of what is perhaps the best known and most useful application of personality constructs to tourism behaviour: Plog's allocentric/psychocentric model. This model is generally regarded as forming a part of the domain known as psychographics which, in turn, is a part of the tourism marketing arena. Psychographic measurement, i.e. using personality items to develop profiles of consumer types, is a young field. It has grown up basically in the last 30 years.

Plog (1987) points out that the early studies tended to use standardised instruments to determine relationships between personality variables and buying behaviour, such as the MMPI, CPI and Allport-Vernon scales, and various measures of persuasibility and other more recent concepts, such as 'yea saying' and 'nay saying' (from Couch and Kenniston 1960) and dogmatism (Rokeach Scale). Most of these studies are said to have offered limited predictability of consumer choice for products because the standardised instruments were developed for basic research purposes rather than for the more focused and limited needs of a market researcher. Plog, however, also makes the point that researchers are now developing scales which are more specific to the needs of the occasion. Thus, there is a greater likelihood that the personality characteristics measured will have some meaningful relationship to consumer behaviour.

Plog (1987) has further made the point that the real impetus to psychographics came from psychologists who developed basic yet useful personality tests. Their fundamental assertion, a necessary precondition for all psychographic research, is that self-report (answering questions) can be reliable and predictive of behaviour. For example, the Allport-Vernon Study of Values is still found to be a useful conceptual tool for market researchers. Plog also points out that the field was given an even greater lift, however, by researchers such as Raymond B. Cattell, who used systematic research techniques and sophisticated statistics to develop his Trait Factor Theory of Personality and the Cattell Personality Scale to support his conclusions. Other powerful instruments emerged, such as the Minnesota Multiphasic Personality Inventory (MMPI), the most widely used diagnostic test employed by clinicians, and the California Psychological Inventory (CPI), a more general measure of personality.

Plog (1972) has put forward a personality theory of tourism behaviour which encompasses two fundamental personality dimensions: allocentricism and psychocentricism. Travellers who are more allocentric are thought to prefer exotic destinations, unstructured vacations rather than packaged tours, and more involvement with local cultures. Psychocentrics, on the other hand, are thought to prefer familiar destinations, packaged tours, and touristy areas. Later, Plog (1979) added an energy dimension which described the desired level of activity preferred by the tourist: high-energy travellers prefer high levels of activity while low-energy travellers prefer fewer activities. Plog (1979) considers the allocentrism/psychocentrism dimension and energy dimension, that is to say independent of each other, to be orthogonal.

A number of studies have now involved examination of allocentrism/ psychocentrism and energy. Plog (1972) has devised a measure of the two dimensions that he has regularly used in market studies. Williams, Ellis and Daniels (1986) have examined the extent to which allocentric and psychocentric travel experience preferences can be used to predict destination preferences. It is said that results of that study generally provided support for Plog's two-dimensional model.

Plog (1987) has made the point that there are many uses for psychographic research. Examples of psychographically relevant topics in travel/leisure research are said to include:

* Destination development — clarifying the concept of a new resort to be developed, the markets to be served, the services and amenities to be provided to visitors, etc.

* Product positioning — focusing a product or service to a greater degree on the needs and psychology of its primary users. Much like an automobile manufacturer, or a food product company, travel/leisure companies must position their products and services to appeal to specific market segments.

* Development of supporting services — determining which services are essential and which are optional for a travel-related company. Essential services must be included, while optional services should be considered only if they are not very costly or they add to the overall marketability of the product.

* Advertising and promotion — focusing the message on the appropriate group of travellers. Their psychology, personal whims, motivations, and basic needs can be appealed to through messages that are highly targeted.

* Packaging — making certain that you not only have the right products and services, but that you have also packaged them appropriately. It is possible that a destination area may have all of the amenities, facilities and activities desired by a group of travellers, but not identified as such. Advertising can get the message out, but the concept must be presented (packaged) in such a way that it fits the customer's perceived needs.

* Master planning — developing a master plan which protects the inherent beauty and attractiveness of a destination, while still meeting the needs of travellers. This requirement is fundamental to all groups concerned with travel and tourism, such as visitors' associations, developers, hotels, airlines, and cruise ship companies.

Plog (1987) has shown that there are a limited number of psychographic/personality dimensions which have been discussed in travel research. These dimensions may be more clearly defined, or recombined in various ways, but they are covered by about eight broad categories. These are listed below and, in each case, there is typically an opposite character type at the other end of the spectrum.

- Venturesomeness — called by a variety of titles, it relates primarily to the type of individual who is more seeking and exploring. In terms of travel destinations, new products, or new marketing concepts, it is this individual who tends to be the first user.
- Pleasure-seeking — the type of person who desires a considerable amount of luxury and comfort in all aspects of travel, transportation carrier services, hotel services, entertainment and other activities.
- Impulsivity — the tendency to want to do something now. Very low on the ability to delay gratification, persons who measure high in this characteristic are more apt to live more for the moment, and will be high spenders. Trip decisions are made quickly, at the last moment, and without much planning.
- Self-confidence — a characteristic growing out of some of the other variables, self-confidence is closely related to the willingness to do unique and very different things, such as selecting the unusual in tour destinations or activities at these destinations.
- Planfulness — an obvious reference to very systematic, planful characteristics in people. Individuals who are strong on this dimension not only will think about and plan their trip well in advance, but will typically look more for bargains and prepackaged tour programs.
- Masculinity — this dimension is sometimes called 'the outdoorsman'. It is the action-oriented man whose primary goal is to seek the outdoors in the very traditional sense (fishing, camping, hunting, field and stream pursuits). This type of person is more likely to travel by car and take many things with him. Wives are often forced into going along with these interests or they are left at home.
- Intellectualism — this characteristic refers to that type of individual who not only possesses highbrow interests (goes to plays, museums, and other cultural activities), but has a heavy orientation towards historical touring. Old historic sites, cultural events, and exploring the undiscovered antecedents of present-day societies are of prime interest to persons dominated by this characteristic.
- People orientation — this is a desire to get close to people through travel and to experience the many cultures of the world. The dimension includes some combination of sociability, lack of organisation (frequently bordering on disorganisation), unique venturesomeness, and some degree of impulsivity.

Criticism and refinement of Plog's model

Nickerson and Ellis (1991) have argued that, despite the general support for Plog's (1972) model, many important questions and refinements remain. One

of these is the source of the allocentrism/psychocentrism and energy dispositions. Are those dispositions learned responses, or are they mostly the result
of relatively stable personality characteristics? The answer to this question
would provide important information for refining Plog's model and for making important decisions in destination marketing. Their 1991 study was an
attempt to examine the extent to which the allocentrism/psychocentrism and
energy dimensions can be explained by using Fiske and Maddi's (1961) activation theory of personality development.

Nickerson and Ellis have found that the model based on activation
theory was generally supported, and that further explanation of travellers'
personalities could be obtained. Plog's (1972) descriptors of allocentrics and
psychocentrics without the energy dimension could be incorporated into a
new activation model of travel personality. The activation model of travel
personality is said to broaden Plog's (1972) original theory by providing more
types of travellers. The personality types can be described in terms of destination preferences, travel companions, interactions with local cultures, degree of
activity participation, and other distinguished characteristics. For example, the
individual who is a high-activation extrovert (allocentric), but with an external
locus of control, would be expected to enjoy cities or popular campgrounds.
This person would enjoy package tourism to new and different places.
Because of the need for variety and tendencies towards extroversion, this
person would believe a package tour could provide all the necessary delights
of travelling without taking risks. This traveller type has been called the vora-
cious tourtaker, meaning that each vacation would involve a package tour to
different destinations.

These findings are said to have additional theoretical, methodological, and
practical dimensions. From a theoretical standpoint, results of this study suggest that personality theories may prove to be useful in explaining tourism
phenomena. Testing of theory and/or models are said to be generally lacking
in tourism research (Cohen 1979a; Hartman 1988). The study by Nickerson
and Ellis thus represents an important contribution in this arena.

Nickerson and Ellis also make the point that confirmation and refinement
of their model would also provide numerous practical implications in terms
of destination development, service positioning, and advertising and promotion. If the managers of a destination desire to attract the high-activation type,
for example, the destination would need to provide variety from everyday
living, a broad range of activities or options from which to choose, and a non-
touristy atmosphere (Plog 1972). Travel destinations might also be more effectively positioned in the market by considering the activation and energy
needs of their primary visitors. Low-activation destinations, for example, might
package their products and services to appeal to this specific market segment
by emphasizing products and services that promote a relaxing atmosphere, a

manageable number of choices, and familiarity through restaurants and hotels that are similar to those with which visitors are accustomed. Comfort and familiarity within the destination should lead to repeat visitation of low-activation traveller types. Finally, Nickerson and Ellis make the point that advertising and promotion may be designed to focus the message on the appropriate group of travellers in terms of their needs for activation and energy. While these are but a few of the possible examples, they are said to demonstrate possible implications of activation theory to managers in tourism and hospitality.

Lee-Hoxter and Lester (1988) have also explored major personality correlates of Plog's dimension of allocentrism-psychocentrism. The Eysenck Personality Inventory (Eysenck and Eysenck 1970) was used here to measure the personality dimensions of neuroticism and extroversion, and it was expected in their study that psychocentrics would obtain higher neuroticism and introversion scores. Responses to the variety of items on how people liked to spend their vacations were summed to give a total allocentrism-psychocentrism score. This score correlated significantly with extroversion but not with neuroticism. The correlations were found to be not significant for males, but the correlation with extroversion was significant for females and close to significance for neuroticism. Thus they found that females with lower neuroticism and higher extroversion scores were more psychocentric than those with higher neuroticism and lower extroversion scores.

Since all travel destinations were said to be foreign (and thus non-psychocentric), Lee-Hoxter and Lester chose three midcentric destinations (Maui, Toronto and Nassau) and three allocentric destinations (Lima, Cairo and Moscow). Scores for the three allocentric destinations were subtracted from scores for the three midcentric destinations. This score correlated with extroversion scores but not with neuroticism scores. The correlation with extroversion was found for females but not for males. The Lee-Hoxter and Lester study found that, for female college students, psychocentrics had lower neuroticism and higher extroversion scores than allocentrics. The association with extroversion was found for both travel destinations and vacation activities, whereas the association with neuroticism was found only for vacation activities, and then only weakly. These results were not found for males. Reasons for the sex difference were not readily apparent to the researchers. The results were moreover the opposite of those generally predicted by Plog. Plog asserted that psychocentrics would be nervous and inhibited, whereas the Lee-Hoxter and Lester study found that psychocentric females were more likely to be stable extroverts. Finally, it should be remembered that the vast majority of respondents were US students who had never travelled abroad, and most of those who had travelled abroad had visited only midcentric countries such as Canada or the Bahamas. Thus, the results might have been very different had the study been conducted using older adults with a variety of travel experiences abroad. However, this study has suggested possible hypotheses for future research.

The following case study has examined two major personality dimensions, the Protestant Work Ethic and Locus of Control, as they jointly assist in the understanding of an applied tourist domain, that of vocational intention.

Tourism/hospitality vocational plans and personality

While relatively little research has been done relating specific personality dimensions to tourism topics such as employment in the tourism/hospitality industry, a great deal of work has now been completed in the investigation of personality domains such as the Protestant Work Ethic and Locus of Control as they relate to the general work context. Furnham (1990) has summarised much of the literature and research surrounding the Protestant Work Ethic as a measurable concept within psychology. The Protestant Work Ethic is typically referred to as a system of beliefs focusing on work and, in particular, the avoidance of idleness and the encouragement of industriousness, the discouragement of waste and the encouragement of frugality, the eschewing of failure and poverty, and the praise of ambition, wealth, and success. In summarising recent research literature, Furnham (1990) has concluded that those who exhibit higher levels of the Protestant Work Ethic are also more likely to be actively involved in and committed to leisure-time pursuits. Thus far, however, little research seems to have been completed examining the relationships between the Protestant Work Ethic and work in specific contexts such as the tourism industry.

Spector (1982) has made the point that personality variables play an important role in the understanding of job motivation and personal work preference. Spector has argued that Locus of Control is perhaps one of the most prominent personality variables that has been studied in a variety of work and organisational settings. Literature on employment in the tourist industry and on job attainment typically focuses on the desirability of a range of characteristics in job success within the tourist industry (Tourism Training Queensland, 1990). An emphasis on previous work experiences, gregariousness, positive attitudes, self-confidence, and an accomplished presentation in the employment interview are all highly valued, with no singular reliance being placed on formal qualifications.

Ross (1990) has investigated the relationship between a set of sociodemographic variables and various work responses in the tourist industry. Six hundred and thirty-four school leavers from the far north Queensland region of Australia were sampled. The major employer in this particular region is the tourism industry, and many of the students sampled would soon be considering this industry as a possible employer. Students were asked whether they would or would not consider the possibility of employment in the tourism industry, were asked whether they would or would not consider further training as a method of acquiring a more lucrative position in the tourism industry, and were asked whether formal qualifications or rather a range of criteria (including practical experience, formal qualifications, presentation, and performance in a job interview) was the critical factor in tourist industry job attainment. The Protestant Work Ethic was measured by the Ho and Lloyd (1984) work ethic scale, and the Locus of Control construct by the Spector (1988) locus of control scale, which was specifically designed for the work context. As well, sociodemographic variables such as sex, number of friends and relatives working in the tourist industry, previous tourist industry work experience, and length of time spent working in the tourist industry were recorded. Forty-four per cent of subjects were male and 56% were female, 28% had previously worked in the tourist industry whereas 72% had not. The mean age of subjects was 16 yrs, with a standard deviation of 1.1. The mean number of friends/relatives in the industry was 5.0 with a standard deviation of 10.1, and the mean number of months working in the industry was 11.0, with a standard deviation of 13.3.

Table 3.1 contains Spearman rho correlations (corrected for ties) between a number of sociodemographic and personality variables, together with the three tourist industry work responses. From this table it can be seen that females were more likely to express an interest in tourist industry work and also express preparedness to complete further studies to obtain a more lucrative tourist industry position. Those students with more friends and relatives working in this industry and who had some previous work experience in this industry were more likely to be associated with the belief that a range of factors accounted for job attainment in the tourist industry rather than simply formal qualifications. The variable length of time working in the tourist industry did not appear to be associated with any of the three work responses. Both personality measures rendered significant correlations. Higher scores on the work ethic scale were associated with a willingness to undertake training and also with the belief in more realistic job attainment criteria. An internal Locus of Control was also associated with each of these tourist industry work responses.

This study has indicated that both sociodemographic and personality variables are related to a willingness to work in the Australian tourism industry, to undergo further training, and to rely upon a realistic range of criteria in obtaining a position in this industry. From these results it may be concluded that women are more likely to evince an interest in employment in the tourist industry and also training for a better position. It is also the case that greater familiarity with the industry either by having more friends and relatives in it or by having some previous experience, albeit mostly part-time for this population, seems to equip students with a more realistic understanding of employment criteria. Also, those students demonstrating higher levels on the Work Ethic were more likely to indicate a willingness to train and have more realistic employment criteria whereas those with an internal Locus of Control are more likely to express an interest in tourist industry work, for retraining and a more pragmatic view of job attainment criteria. Further research might explore these personality dimensions in a variety of tourist and leisure contexts throughout the tourism world. A greater understanding of the personality of potential employees may assist not only in the area of labour-force planning but also in career guidance wherein the supply of more accurate industry information can result in a greater success in job attainment or the choice of alternative career paths.

Personality and ethical tourism

Hultsman (1995) has argued the necessity of considering a paradigm of ethicality in which tourism services and behaviour might be grounded. Such a paradigmatic framework is seen as being distinct from and as a potentially useful precursor to attempts to develop operational standards or codes of ethics for various facets of the delivery of tourism services. Hultsman has called for an operational perspective of ethics wherein the need to develop an ethical code of behaviour for international tourism services is central. Such a code, he suggests, would help ensure that the ways in which tourism goods and services are marketed meet or exceed widely accepted industry standards and practices (e.g. standards for truth in advertising). Such codes of ethical standards covering various facets of tourism goods and services delivery would seem according to Hultsman to be warranted, both for the enhancement of professionalism implicit in them and to help provide consumers with a sense of assurance that they are being treated fairly.

Ethics might at first blush seem an unusual topic to consider in relation to a discussion in personality and tourism. However, appropriate ethical groundings for behaviour in contexts such as the tourism/hospitality industry are increasingly seen as important topics, and it is argued that the antecedents of such behaviour need to be understood within the context of basic personality processes. The concept of ethics (both as philosophical inquiry into values, and as practical application of moral behaviour) is illuminated by two issues. First, as Aristotle cautioned, one cannot demand greater clarity than a subject allows; ethics are said to be not discernible per se. As with aesthetic

Table 3.1 Spearman rho rank order correlations corrected for ties between sociodemographic and personality variables, and tourist industry work responses

	Tourist Industry Work Interest	Retraining Option	Job Attainment Criteria
Sex	.18#	.20*	.09
Number of friends/ relations working in tourist industry	.05	.02	.16#
Previous work experience in tourist industry	–.08	–.05	.16+
Length of time working in tourist industry	–.04	.05	–.01
Protestant Work Ethic	.08	.12+	.12+
Locus of Control	–.15#	–.21*	–.16#

*p < .001, #p < .01, +p < .05

From Ross, 1990

judgments, however, it is possible to reach ethical perspectives from the experience of emotions, as one may feel morally moved when witnessing an act of kindness or cruelty. Second and in a related context, ethics are said to reside between the 'is' and the 'ought'. Ethics and the feelings and values on which they are based, are subjective. They may thus be seen to emanate from the domain of the personality (Hultsman, 1995).

Hultsman also calls for broader discussions of ethics in tourism and hospitality policy-making, and argues for a discussion of how philosophy and ethics might be used to develop a framework for tourism decision-making that might lead towards more socially responsible and sensitive tourism development. He points out that the International Institute for Quality and Ethics in Service and Tourism has produced an edited text that discusses ethics across a broad range of topics relevant to the hospitality industry in the interest of encouraging more writing about the topics of ethics and to encourage professional schools to begin more in-depth teaching of the topic.

It has also been suggested by Hultsman that an ethical framework for tourism service delivery can be developed with an eye to the conceptual meaning of tourism. The ethical framework proposed can be considered primarily from the experiential personality perspective of the tourist. Within this experiential personality context, it is suggested that what needs to be perpetuated is a spirit of tourism services delivery necessary to allow tourists to find meaning in and derive benefits from activities in which they engage. Hultsman is thus advocating that tourism services should be delivered in a principled manner. The underlying premise of this facet of 'just tourism' is that some generally understood and basic ethicality is fundamental and necessary to the evolution of tourism as a recognised and legitimate profession. For Hultsman the question of what constitutes acceptable ethical behaviour in the delivery of tourism services (i.e. what is 'generally understood and basic ethicality') is at the heart of this aspect of 'just tourism'. However, it is here suggested that an ethical orientation among tourism people be conceptualised as having its foundation point in individual interpersonal functioning and thus personality processes. Thus changes in ethical conduct will emanate from basic personality dimensions.

Tourist group holiday decision-making

Personality is a notion that has been applied not only to the individual or to intra-psychological processes, but also to processes that involve groups of people. Thornton, Shaw and Williams (1997) have examined the influence that children have on the behaviour of tourist groups while on holidays. They hold that the role of children has generally been under-researched and also, probably because of this, undervalued. They have employed a diary-based space-time budget survey to collect information on the activities of tourist groups holidaying in Cornwall in the UK. They found that children had considerable influence over the behaviour of their respective groups. This influence was manifested not only in the assuaging of their immediate physical needs such as meal arrangements and sleep times, but also in their ability to negotiate with their parents and caregivers. Thornton et al. note that overall it was found that holiday activities were heavily group based, even when groups included teenage children. The personality of the group, it would thus seem, played a dominant role in behavioural outcomes.

They suggest that this cohesiveness evident among groups has important implications for the ability of children to influence the activities of the group. One illustration of this influence concerned possible disappointment by children in some tourist product. Thornton et al. found that any such experience which fails to satisfy a child will have a strong knock-on effect upon parents. Thornton *et al.* stress the important role of group decisions in purchasing tourism products while on holidays. They have concluded that there is a clear need for theories in this context which are sensitive to the subtle influence of group decision-making, together with the demonstrated ability of children to influence and change group holiday behaviour.

Summary

This chapter has examined the notion of personality as it has relevance for tourism, and has shown how the concept of personality may be of central importance in understanding a great deal of tourism behaviour. The chapter has provided a coverage of some of the basics of personality from mainstream psychology, and then presented one of the most prominent applications of personality to tourism behaviour, that of Plog's allocentrism/psychocentrism model. The chapter presented a recent study exploring personality dimensions such as the Protestant Work Ethic and Locus of Control to vocational intent in the tourism/hospitality industry. Finally, the chapter has introduced the notion of ethical tourism and also group decision-making from a personality perspective.

CHAPTER 3   DISCUSSION TOPICS

How has the word personality been defined?

Name the major ways in which allocentrics and psychocentrics are said to differ.

Describe some of the uses for psychographic research.

Discuss a refinement or extension of Plog's Allocentric/Psychocentric model.

How might the study of ethics enhance tourist experiences?

How might tourism group processes affect tourist behaviour?

4

Attitudes and the Tourist

LEARNING OBJECTIVES

An understanding of:

- The basic components of the mental/emotional phenomenon commonly referred to as an attitude.
- Applications of this psychological construct to tourist behaviour.
- Two major research approaches within the tourism domain that have employed this construct: VALS and LOV.
- Attitudes and their relationships to travel decisions among senior citizens.
- Prestige and travel.
- Values and tourist behaviour.

This chapter will focus on attitudes, and how they influence and are related to tourism behaviour. It will commence with a coverage of attitudes as they are conceptualised within the general social psychology literature. The chapter will then explore the application of such concepts to tourism by way of an exposition of a number of recent major studies of attitudes and tourism. The chapter will then provide a presentation of a major study involving attitudes, satisfaction and tourism among seniors. The chapter will conclude with a coverage of prestige attitudes and also values as they relate to the behaviour of tourists.

Attitudes

This section will introduce a number of very basic propositions which summarise attitudes. These propositions have been adumbrated by Eiser (1986) thus:

1   Attitudes are subjective experiences. This assumption is basic to most definitions, although some writers, notably Bem (1967) are said to regard

people's statements about their attitudes as inferences from observations of their own behaviour.

2   Attitudes are experiences of some issue or object. This point is rarely acknowledged explicitly. Not all experiences qualify as attitudes. Attitudes are not simply 'moods' or 'affective reactions' presumed to be somehow caused by external stimuli. Reference to some issue or object is said to be part of the experience.

3   Attitudes are experiences of some issue or object in terms of an evaluative dimension. If we have an attitude towards an object we do not simply experience it, we experience it as more or less desirable, or better or worse, to some degree. While it is accepted that attitudes involve evaluations, there is less than unanimity over whether attitudes are only evaluative. Even among those who define attitudes more inclusively, though, there is a preparedness to allow attitudes to be measured along an evaluative continuum.

4   Attitudes involve evaluative judgements. This point follows on from the third proposition above. However, caution is needed in what we read into the term 'judgement'. It is an empirical question how much a particular person's attitude to (or evaluative judgement of) some object in some situation involves deliberate, conscious appraisal of that object, as opposed to, for example, an over learned conditioned response.

5   Attitudes may be expressed through language. Attitudes may be expressed non-verbally to some extent, but we could only apply a very impoverished conception of attitude to a species which did not have speech. Ordinary language is replete with words containing an element of evaluation (see Osgood, Suci and Tannenbaum 1957).

6   Expressions of attitude are, in principle, intelligible. This is both the most obvious and most intangible fact about attitudes. When other people express their attitudes, we can understand them. We may not know why they feel as they do, but, within limits, we know what they feel.

7   Attitudes are communicated. Expressions of attitudes are not simply intelligible, they are typically made so as to be perceived and understood by others. In other words the expression of attitude is a social act that presupposes an audience by whom that expression may be understood. How the presence, kind and size of the audience may affect the expression of attitude is said to be an empirical question.

8   Different individuals can agree and disagree in their attitudes. This proposition is dependent both on the notion that attitudes can be expressed in language (since language permits notation) and on the notion that attitudes have a public reference.

9   People who hold different attitudes towards an object will differ in what

they believe is true or false about that object. The possibility of attitudinal agreement and disagreement implies that people will interpret attitude statements as having truth values that are in principle determinable through interaction with the attitude object. However, it is not necessarily the case that attitudes are formed on the basis of prior investigation of relevant facts. The relationship between factual beliefs and evaluation is an empirical question.

10 Attitudes are predictably related to social behaviour. This is among the most intriguing assumptions concerning attitudes, and has the following implications: (a) if people generally showed no consistency between their verbally expressed attitudes and other social behaviour, it would be difficult to know what such verbal expression meant; (b) though people may be motivated to obtain, approach, support, etc. objects they evaluate as positive, this is unlikely to be the only motive relevant to social behaviour, and its relative importance in any context is an empirical question; (c) to talk of attitudes causing behaviour (or vice versa) can often beg questions concerning the nature of the intervening processes.

Attitudes and tourism

This section will provide an examination of two major recent expositions of attitudes and their conceptual value in respect to the understanding of two dimensions of tourism behaviour: attitudes and tourist destination choices, and consumer value constructs.

Attitudes and destination choice

Um and Crompton (1990, 1991) have argued that the image of a place as a pleasure travel destination is derived from attitudes towards the destination's perceived tourism attributes. They make the point that potential travellers generally have limited knowledge about the attributes of a destination which they have not previously visited. For this reason, the image and attitude dimensions of a place as a travel destination are said likely to be critical elements in the destination choice process, irrespective of whether or not they are true representations of what that place has to offer.

Um and Crompton make the point that attitudes have been one of the most popular variables used in the consumer behaviour field to try and predict consumer choice behaviour. Several multi-attribute models have been developed which measure attitudes and attempt to relate attitudes to behaviour (e.g. Fishbein and Ajzen 1975; Rosenberg 1956). They point out that a substantial body of literature using these models has emerged, and one of its salient conclusions is that when situational constraints are specified and integrated into consumer choice models, their predictive power is enhanced.

(Belk 1975; Hansen 1976; Park 1978; Tybout and Hauser 1981). Multi-attribute models which ignore this component are said unlikely to accurately reflect consumers' choice processes. In the context of tourism, Crompton (1977) suggested that destination choice should be conceptualised as being a function of the interaction between pragmatic constraints such as time, money, skills and destination images. More recently, they point out that this approach was endorsed by Woodside and Lysonski (1989) in their general model of traveller choice.

Destination choice has been conceptualised as having two phases by Crompton (1977). The first is a generic phase which addresses the fundamental issue of whether or not to have a holiday at all. Once the decision in favour of a holiday is made, the second phase is concerned with where to go. A framework of pleasure travel destination choice has been developed by Um and Crompton (1990, 1991) to provide a context for the study. Their model identifies and integrates five sets of processes which are presented as flows: (a) the formation of subjective beliefs about destination attributes in the awareness set, through passive information catching or incidental learning; (b) a decision to undertake a pleasure trip (initiation of a destination choice process) which includes consideration of situational constraints; (c) evolution of an evoked set from the awareness set of destinations; (d) the formation of subjective beliefs about the destination attributes of each alternative in the evoked set of destinations, through active solicitation of information; and (e) selection of a specific travel destination. The framework also identifies three constructs which evolve from these five processes. They are awareness set, evoked set, and travel destination selection (Um and Crompton, 1990, 1991).

Consumer values

This section examines values as they relate to consumer behaviour. It will address what is possibly the most debated issue in this area, that of methodological precision in the measurement and prediction of consumer behaviour by way of the measurement of consumer values. Kahle, Beatty and Homer (1986) have made the point that methodology has been of considerable interest to researchers (e.g. Beatty et al., 1985; Reynolds, Clawson and Vinson, Scott and Lamont (1977). Clawson and Vinson (1978) imply that progress in methodological issues is crucial for understanding the relationship between consumer behaviour and values. This section therefore covers two conceptually different ways of measuring values.

I. Values and lifestyle
Kahle, Beatty and Homer (1986) argue that one of the more useful developments in values methodology in recent years has been the Values and Life Style (VALS) methodology developed at SRI International by Mitchell (1983). They point out that it started from the theoretical base of Maslow's (1954) needs

hierarchy and the concept of social character (Riesman, Glazer and Denney 1950). Questions were identified through statistical and theoretical means as useful in classifying people into one of nine life style groups. These questions are said to include various specific and general attitude statements and several demographic items. The life style groups in the United States are said to include survivors (4 per cent), sustainers (7 per cent), belongers (35 per cent), emulators (9 per cent), achievers (22 per cent), I-am-me (5 per cent), experiential (7 per cent), societally conscious (9 per cent), and integrated (2 per cent). A proprietary system of weighting questions for classification was developed using data from a national probability sample of 1,635 Americans and their spouses/mates (1,078) who responded to an SRI International mail survey in 1980. This study also included a number of questions about consumer behaviour. Although many studies have apparently applied VALS methodology (e.g. Homan 1984), only the 1980 study results would seem to have been made public for quantitative inspection.

Kahle, Beatty and Homer (1986) point out that from the 1980 VALS survey (Mitchell 1983) we know the quantitative results of fewer than 90 questions, although Homan (1984) reports that over 800 questions were asked. That 90 includes the 30+ algorithm items (i.e. items used to classify people into VALS types). Thus, only about 60 reported items were criterion variables to be cross-tabulated with the VALS categories. Even assuming that all 90 reported differences in Mitchell (1983) were indeed statistically significant (though no tests were reported), it should be remembered that with 800 items, 40 would be significant at the 0.05 level purely by chance, by normal random fluctuations in data. Thus, Kahle, Beatty and Homer (1986) believe it is possible that some of these reported findings in Mitchell (1983) are less important than others. One way to identify robust differences is through replication.

II. List of Values

Kahle, Beatty and Homer (1986) point out that one alternative to VALS is the List of Values (LOV), which was developed by researchers at the University of Michigan Survey Research Centre (Kahle 1983; Veroff, Douvan and Kulka 1981). LOV it is pointed out was developed from a theoretical base of Feather's (1975), Maslow's (1954), and Rokeach's (1973) work on values in order to assess adaptation to various roles through value fulfilment. It is tied most closely to social adaptation theory (Kahle 1983, 1984a). Subjects would see a list of nine values, including self-respect, security, warm relationships with others, sense of accomplishment, self-fulfilment, sense of belonging, being well respected, fun and enjoyment in life, and excitement. These values have been used to classify people on Maslow's (1954) hierarchy, and they relate more closely to the values of life's major roles (i.e. marriage, parenting, work, leisure, daily consumption) than do the values in the Rokeach (1973) Value

Survey (Beatty *et al.* 1985). In the LOV method, Kahle, Beatty and Homer point out that subjects have been asked to identify their two most important values (Kahle 1983; Veroff *et al.* 1981) or to rank the values (Beatty *et al.* 1985), as Rokeach (1973) prefers with his value survey. The values, they argue, could also be evaluated through paired comparison (Reynolds and Jolly 1980) or rating approaches (Munson 1984).

Kahle, Beatty and Homer also point out that VALS and LOV have several obvious similarities — for example, the VALS classification of achievers and the LOV classification of sense of accomplishment; or the VALS classification of belongers and the LOV classification of sense of belonging. In some instances the overlap seems logically unlikely, such as the VALS classification of societally conscious or the LOV classification of self-respect, because the groups are semantically quite different. Both methods, it is said, have identified an inner-outer distinction. In VALS the distinction is called outer-directed vs inner-directed, but it derives from Riesman *et al.*'s (1950) concept of other-directed (Holman 1984). The outer-directed groups are said to include achievers, emulators, and belongers, while the inner-directed groups are said to include the societally conscious, experientials, and I-am-me. In the LOV research the distinction is said to be between internal vs external locus of control (Rotter 1966); the external values include sense of belonging, being well respected, and security, while the internal values include the rest. LOV theory also notes the importance of people in value fulfilment. Kahle, Beatty and Homer further point out that values can be fulfilled through interpersonal relationships (warm relationships with others, sense of belonging), personal factors (self-respect, being well respected, self-fulfilment), or apersonal things (sense of accomplishment, security, excitement, fun and enjoyment in life). Although this discussion is said to imply that a factor analysis would show two primary factors in LOV, future research may show that the factor structure is possibly contextual.

Both techniques of measurement have been carefully considered by Kahle, Beatty and Homer within the context of life span developmental psychology. Whereas in VALS the individual is viewed as going from worse to better (e.g. integrated people are better than sustainers), within the LOV framework no such expectation is said to exist. Mitchell describes the apparent anomaly in VALS of the oldest group being the lowest developmentally as the result of people who 'slipped back' (1983, p. 47), whereas within the LOV framework maturation is said not to be conceptualised in this manner. Finally, Kahle, Beatty and Homer say that in LOV the identity of a better value is contextual, and it is believed that, for both LOV and VALS, identified age difference could be due to the obvious factor of age, but could also be due to development, history, biological influences, situation influences, cohort effects, or interactions of these various factors.

Kahle, Beatty and Homer (1986) have compared and contrasted the VALS and LOV methodologies and by implication the utility of their underlying theories. They have concluded that the LOV had greater predictive ability than did VALS in the context of consumer behaviour and tourism, and accounts for more consumer behaviour variance than does VALS. In conclusion, LOV and VALS have received considerable research attention in the US, and have been found to be useful instruments within a marketing context. Both would seem to offer considerable future potential in the context of tourism research.

Attitudes and seniors' decisions to travel

Zimmer, Brayley and Seale (1995) have studied the differences between older adults who travel and those who do not, as well as their destination choices. Attitudes emerged as an important variable type in this study. The travel destinations of Manitoba seniors were found to be quite diverse. From the results of their research it was clear that the characteristics of those who choose nearby destinations differ in a number of ways from those who choose to travel farther. Factors such as income, education, rural residency, willingness to spend money on recreation, and health status influence the choice of destination. Urban residents who were better educated, had more money, and were predisposed towards spending money on recreation tend to travel farther from home, while those with health problems tended to travel to nearby US destinations.

Interesting comparisons were also made by Zimmer, Brayley and Seale between factors that influence whether a senior was a traveller and those that determined travel destination among the group classified as travellers. Place of residency, rural or urban, was found not to influence the choice to travel. It was found, however, to have a substantial influence on the chosen destination. This was also found to be true in regard to attitudes to life satisfaction. Zimmer, Brayley and Seale (1995) argue that to the travel marketer, this presents a challenge and raises the question 'Can you alter travel behaviour by altering those factors that seem to influence it?' They conclude that there were other variables that may also be predictors of travel behaviour among the elderly as well as the ones used in this analysis. The findings of their investigation point to some factors in which the travel manager or marketer may or may not be able to produce positive change. They conclude that while one cannot alter place of residence (rural or urban) to effect such changes in destination choice, education, which was identified as the second most powerful influence of travel behaviour, can be managed to produce some desired travel results. Education (which includes information through advertising) is said to provide an awareness of other cultures, history, and geography that may serve to influence interest in and attitudes towards travel. Thus, travel-related education as an attitude-change agent has been found to be an effective process for encouraging the seniors market to travel farther afield. Travel marketers, it is said, can influence travel behaviour by increasing the perceived income of the market or by reducing its influence through establishment of a sense of value and purchasing power in the minds of the would-be consumers. Thus it may be concluded that attitude change is an important tool for travel marketers.

Prestige attitudes and tourism

Riley (1995) has studied prestige related attitudinal constructs and their role as mediators of travel decision-making. Riley has made the point that the relationship between prestige and leisure travel has received little empirical attention, and for the most part, even the more encompassing social recognition concepts of status and class have been neglected. Although people can readily identify leisure travel they consider prestige-worthy, a key problem, according to Riley, is the lack of understanding about the differentiation between worthy and unworthy leisure travel behaviours. Despite intuitive knowledge of travel behaviours that might generate prestige conference, there is said to be little understanding of the defining qualities that underpin these behaviours. Furthermore, there is said to be little knowledge of the relationship between the conferer of prestige and the person upon whom the honourable social recognition is bestowed.

Riley holds that prestige-worthiness can be interpreted from episodes that occurred prior to travel; during the travel engagement phase (including travel to and from destinations); and in the post-travel phase. In each of these phases, prestige-worthiness can be related to features and attractions at the destinations, and from the initiatives of travellers. Pre-travel, destination-attraction prestige can often be a function of prior media information. Prestige also existed in the tourists' ability to manage resources that allowed them to travel. Moreover, according to Riley, resource management, traveller adventurism, and windfall opportunities of time and money differentiate the behaviours of travellers conferred with prestige. Travel engagement prestige has been interpreted by Riley from the destination observations of indigenous cultures, viewing unique natural attractions, meeting noteworthy people, overcoming destination constraints, exemplary guest treatment, and visitation to symbolic centres. Spontaneity and unplanned wanderlust are noted as traveller initiated instances of prestige. Frequency and variety of travel experiences are also noted instances that differentiated the prestige conferred upon travellers by others. Instances of post-travel prestige conference are noted by Riley in the display of mementos and artefacts from destinations visited.

Riley further identifies underlying dimensions of prestige leisure travel. Two underlying dimensions of prestige are outlined. The first dimension is labelled relative exclusivity and the second dimension is labelled personal and/or empathetic desirability. Neither relative exclusivity, nor personal or empathetic desirability are thought to be singularly sufficient to conclude the prestige-worthiness of leisure travel behaviours. Riley also highlights the exclusivity dimension of prestige-worthy leisure travel. The exclusivity dimension of prestige is said to be related to experiences that were considered to be minimally accessible, out-of-the-ordinary, or sometimes unique. Without the dimension of exclusivity, the travel behaviours are said to pass unnoticed among other known leisure travel experiences. With the dimension of exclusivity being evident, prestige-worthy leisure travel is said to be conspicuous when compared with other leisure travel.

Riley also calls attention to the relative nature of exclusivity. The exclusivity of prestige-worthy leisure travel episodes is believed to be relative to the other leisure travel knowledge held by the informants. The relativity of exclusivity is the result of informants' comparative exercises concerning: 1. Self Referencing — an informant's perception of the leisure travel episode compared to their previous (or projected) leisure travel experiences; 2. Travel Opportunity Referencing — an informant's expectations or perceptions of a traveller's everyday behaviour compared to their expected leisure travel behaviour. When self referencing, the observed travel behaviour is considered exclusive when the evaluator compares it to, and perceives a deficiency in, their own travel experiences. Deficiencies are said to occur for many reasons: some pertain to a lack of personal travel opportunity, while others are credited to an inability to undertake the vast array of leisure travel opportunities available.

Finally, Riley enunciates a desirability dimension of prestige-worthy leisure travel. Desirability is said to be manifest in two forms. The first type of desirability is labelled personal and the second empathetic. The former is an expressed desire to fulfil observed leisure travel opportunities not yet undertaken by the informant. The second form of desirability pertains to travel that is not personally desirable for informants, although they do recognise them to be desirable for the traveller involved. Here, Riley believes the informant has an empathetic understanding about leisure travel considered desirable by the traveller. For leisure travel to be empathetically desirable, the informant needs to be cognisant and accepting of the traveller's desires. In conclusion, Riley (1995) has identified a major attitudinal construct, prestige, and has also explored some of the concomitants of its operation. It is suggested that this construct has considerable, but thus far largely unexplored value in the understanding of tourist behaviour.

Values and tourist behaviour

Thrane (1997) has explored the role of values in the understanding of tourist behaviour. The point is made by Thrane that values ought to be considered as important criteria in the understanding of tourist phenomena. Using a Norwegian sample, Thrane has examined the relevance of two fundamental value dimensions (materialistic-idealistic and modern-traditional) in order to discriminate among tourism motives and also behaviour. It has been found that both of the value dimensions were associated with a variety of variables including tourist motives and behaviour. Other predicted variables found to be important in the understanding of the values-motives relationships were socio-demographic variables such as age, sex and level of formal education. Thrane makes the important point that basic values held by travellers and potential travellers have considerable explanatory value in regard to factors such as tourist motives and behavioural intent.

Summary

This chapter has sought to provide understandings of one of the most fundamental topics in applied psychology, that of attitudes, particularly as they shed light on tourist behaviour. Attitudes have been seen to be of considerable value in the understanding and prediction of tourist behaviour. In particular this chapter has presented two major attitude instruments — the VALS and the LOV which are in currency in the tourism research arena. The chapter then concluded with recent studies which involved attitudes and their relationships to travel decision-making among senior citizens, travel prestige attitude constructs, and fundamental values and tourist behaviour.

CHAPTER 4 DISCUSSION TOPICS

What are the basic distinguishing features of attitudes?

From which sources do beliefs about destination attributes emanate?

Crompton (1977) conceptualises destination choice as having two phases. Name and describe each phase.

Describe similarities and differences between VALS and LOV.

How might travel behaviour among seniors be modified?

Discuss the role of prestige in travel decision-making.

Discuss the explanatory role of values.

5

Environment and the Tourist

LEARNING OBJECTIVES

An understanding of:

- The value of environmental perceptions within the tourism context.
- The specific contribution of cognitive mapping in understanding tourist behaviour.
- The impacts of environmental manipulation in areas such as queuing, so as to maximise tourism satisfaction.
- Legitimacy considerations in ecotourism.

This chapter will provide an understanding of some of the major notions that underpin the area of environmental psychology and tourism. The chapter will demonstrate that conceptualisations of the environment from the discipline of psychology provide major understandings of tourism behaviour. It will commence with an introduction to research into the environmental images of tourism, and will then include a coverage of the domain of cognitive mapping and tourism. Other environmental areas covered will include tourism queues. The chapter will conclude with a coverage of the importance of communication skills within environmental education efforts as well as legitimacy considerations in ecotourism.

Environmental images and tourism

The perception of the environment has been subjected to extensive research scrutiny within disciplines such as environmental psychology (Ittelson 1973) and geography (Tuan 1974). A number of commentators have now considered cognitive mapping procedures within the context of the study of tourism (see Britton 1979; Pearce 1981). Downs and Stea (1977) advance the argument that tourism and cognitive maps are very closely linked. All forms of travel, it is said, involve some form of environmental cognition in that people seek out and locate destinations and attractions. As will be seen in Chapter Six, image is basically a mental representation of an object, person, place, or event which is not physically in front of the individual. It is generally argued that cognitive maps may be conceptualised as a particular type of image employed to understand the surrounding environment.

Cognitive maps and tourist experiences

Walmsley and Jenkins (1991) have pointed out that very few researchers have looked at the cognitive maps that tourists have of the areas that they visit. This they find surprising for two reasons. First, the study of short-term, temporary visitors to an area has the potential to contribute to an understanding of environmental learning generally because it could lead to insights into how individuals come to assimilate the new and the unfamiliar. Second, understanding of the way in which tourists come to know resort areas has significant applied value to those concerned with the promotion and commercial viability of tourist attractions, especially as first-time visitors to a resort area are often faced within formation overload when confronted with a plethora of data (e.g. road signs, motel signs, information boards, advertising). Many tourists are said to arrive at a resort area with 'vague to nonexistent cognitive maps of its environmental construction, content, pathways and borders' (Guy, Curtis and Crotts 1990). They then develop some minimal level of environmental learning in order to access the attractions and facilities that are available.

Walmsley and Jenkins point out that Pearce (1977) was one of the first researchers to explore the cognitive maps of tourists. Focusing on landmarks, paths, and districts, Pearce used an experimental design based on sex (male/female), length of stay (2-6 days), and accommodation (central/peripheral) to investigate the environmental knowledge of first-time visitors to Oxford. Data were generated via sketch maps. Pearce showed that cognitive maps were quick to develop: even by the second day in Oxford, subjects had basic cognitive maps in place. Moreover, there was said to be distinct evidence of environmental learning to the extent that the number of landmarks, paths and districts increased over time: over a period of 2-6 days, landmarks on average increased in number from 7 to 9, paths from 4 to 6, and districts from 2 to 3. The ratio of districts to paths to landmarks was consistent (at approximately 1:2:3), suggesting that the maps as a whole became more complex rather than any one element becoming dominant.

Walmsley and Jenkins point out that Pearce (1981) found evidence of learning in a study of how tourists came to know a route along which they travelled in Northern Australia. A 340 km trip from Townsville to Cairns was investigated. Subjects were presented with an outline map of the area (on which were included the two towns and the coastline) and asked to draw the route that they had followed. As before, the numbers of landmarks, paths, and districts were used as measures of knowledge. The results indicated that targeted variables have an important influence on cognitive maps: drivers with better knowledge levels than passengers, and travellers familiar with the route were better oriented than their first- and second-time counterparts. Age, too, was important to the extent that older subjects made more labelling errors than younger subjects. As with the earlier study, Walmsley *et al.* point out that Pearce found no difference between the maps drawn by males and females, except for a tendency for females to report fewer paths in the case of the Oxford sample.

Walmsley and Jenkins (1991) maintain that mental maps can be analysed in two ways: quantitatively (a count of the features included on the maps) and qualitatively (an examination of the way or style in which information is portrayed). They cite Lynch's (1960) early work which suggested that there are five components to images of urban environments: paths which comprise the channels along which people move; edges which serve as barriers to movement; districts which are relatively large areas of a city with an identifiable character; nodes which are foci for travel and places that individuals actually enter; and landmarks which are reference points used in navigation. The existence of these building blocks has, it is argued, been confirmed in a great many subsequent studies. For analytic purposes, they argue that it is possible to count the number of paths, nodes, edges, landmarks and districts on each map. When this is done, it soon becomes apparent that edges are relatively infrequent. There were, basically, only two found by Walmsley and Jenkins in a study of the Australian city of Coffs Harbour (railway, coastline). Both of these are such prominent features that their presence/absence did not serve to differentiate among maps. Problems of a different kind were encountered with nodes. This was regarded as the most problematical of Lynch's categories in that identification of nodes really requires knowledge of the purposive behaviour of the subjects under study. Whether a place is a node (and is entered) or just a landmark (and used for navigation) cannot easily be discerned from the map alone. Churches may be argued to be a case in point, according to Walmsley and Jenkins.

Walmsley and Jenkins (1991) have found that the counting of paths, landmarks, and districts gives a simple quantitative measure of the content of maps. Despite its apparent specificity, however, such counting is said to offer no more than a coarse measurement because, particularly in the case of paths and districts, the number of features present does not accurately indicate the extent of knowledge. Paths vary in length, districts in size. For example, one map might contain six paths but be a much poorer and less extensive representation of reality than one containing three paths. Even landmarks are said to vary from minor features of the streetscape (signs) to major landforms (a lookout). Analysis of the content of mental maps therefore is said to present problems. Table 5.1 provides insights into the way the two groups of business tourists conceptualised Coffs Harbour.

Table 5.1 Mental map content for different personality groups

	Mean number of items shown on maps			
	Experiment 1 Locus of control		Experiment 2 Activity	
	Low scores* internal	High scores* external	Low scores* sitter	High scores* searcher
Landmarks	6.4	5.8	2.3	3.2
Districts	4.3	3.5	2.4	2.3
Paths	4.4	4.4	3.3	4.9

* Scores were designated as high or low on the basis of whether they were above or below the mean described by Rotter (1966) and Eysenck and Wilson (1976).

Source: Walmsley and Jenkins (1991)

This, they admit, is a relatively unsophisticated calibration, but it does facilitate a simple examination of the influence of these particular personality traits. As Table 5.1 shows, in the case of locus of control there was a marked difference between the high and low groups in both the number of landmarks and the number of districts on the maps. Specifically Walmsley and Jenkins found that those with an external locus of control included fewer landmarks and districts on their maps. This is in accord with the rationale advanced for the study of locus of control as a personality trait likely to influence environmental cognition. They conclude that perhaps this suggests a rather passive encountering of the environment by these people, with relatively few features being remembered. Table 5.1 also shows that, in terms of activity, there was a pronounced tendency for more active personalities to include more paths as well as more landmarks. This is in accord with the prima facie argument put above: active personalities appear to put considerable emphasis on paths.

Walmsley and Jenkins conclude that the personality traits of activity and locus of control seem to have a bearing on mental maps. However, the degree of influence varies between the components of the maps, suggesting that mapping style may itself be influenced by such traits.

Walmsley and Jenkins point out that Appleyard (1970) has proposed that mental mapping style can be examined by categorising maps as either sequential (paths and nodes, and therefore linkages, dominant) or spatial (landmarks and districts dominant, with linkages no more than schematic). In Appleyard's view, sequential maps usually dominate in the approximate ratio of 3:1. Anchor point theory, as proposed by Golledge (1978), argues, for example, that people learn landmarks first, then paths linking landmarks, and then districts around groups of landmarks. Walmsley and Jenkins argue that this might explain why their 1991 study (where the subjects were short-term visitors with relatively little prior knowledge of Coffs Harbour) contained rather more spatial maps than has been found to be the case with similar studies of long-term residents. The populations used for this study were at an early stage in the learning process and thus relied to a considerable degree on landmarks. Walmsley and Jenkins conclude that the personality traits of locus of control and activity might well have a bearing on the mental maps that tourists develop of resort areas. Specifically, how tourists score on scales measuring these two traits seems to influence both the features of the landscape that they note in their mental maps and the style of the maps. Certainly the influence of personality on tourist behaviour appears to be worthy of further investigation and within a variety of contexts. Among the more obvious extensions of Walmsley and Jenkins's work are the exploration of other personality traits that might be related to mental mapping, as well as the study of populations other than business tourists.

Tourist queues

Queues are a very common feature of larger tourist attractions, and a phenomenon that can inspire much discontent and negative emotion in many tourists. Pearce (1989) has provided a theoretical understanding of this increasingly common generator of criticism among visitors to a tourism or leisure site. He has argued that in order to begin to understand the psychological needs and processes operating within a population of waiting visitors, it is valuable to review some earlier work by psychologists in this area. The work of Mann and Taylor (1969), and Mann (1977) is said to represent one useful line of enquiry tackling social and cognitive features implicated in people's in-line behaviour. Mann and Taylor (1969) reported the results of three separate naturalistic observation studies where people were waiting respectively for football tickets, Batman shirts and chocolate bars. They predicted that people faced with the possibility of not obtaining a ticket (or prize) will be biased in their estimation of queue length. Pearce reports that they have identified potential biases in people's motivation for continuing to stand in line, and hypothesised that people in line after the 'critical point' (i.e. where the supply of there source could be exhausted) might tend to underestimate their position in that line. The results collected for a line waiting for football tickets were consistent with the interpretation of a defensive or self-justifying position for remaining among the latter members of the queue. Pearce notes that the researchers tentatively considered other explanations of the data (for example, perhaps the accuracy of estimates of line lengths declines disproportionately with the larger queue sizes or perhaps more rounding down of the estimates accounted for the under-estimates of the later queues) — first overestimating the obstacle (in this case the speed at which the queue is moving) and paying heightened attention to the changes which separate the person from the end goal. Fraisse (1963) observes that the common experience of waiting five minutes for someone to come can seem much longer whereas watching an enjoyable five minute television program can seem to have taken much less time. Fraisse argues that the cliché 'time flies when we are happy' is best understood by conceptualising it as time is unnoticed when we are happy, and it is the process of not paying attention to time which makes it pass quickly.

Pearce (1989) also reports that several studies, some conducted over half a century ago, confirm Fraisse's arguments. For example, Axel (1924) asked students to estimate time periods ranging from 15-30 seconds. Some of his subjects did nothing, others were asked to tap a pencil on the desk, others crossed out figures, solved anagrams or worked on complex puzzles. As task complexity increased, time estimation decreased. Additionally, the number of pure guesses rose as task complexity increased, confirming the view that distracting people from the passage of time makes them less aware of its duration. Other studies have confirmed that people who are highly motivated provide briefer time estimates. Many perspectives in psychology emphasise the need for people to operate at an optimum level of information processing — having to deal with too much information is stress inducing, having to deal with too little information also produces stress through the process of lack of control and its consequences of boredom and fatigue. Pearce believes that typically queue members suffer from a lack of information in their environment. They are unsure of how long they will be waiting, they are uncertain as to how crowded the attraction/feature will be when they arrive at the end of the queue and, as discussed before, they are often unable to estimate accurately the number of people in the queue or the time they have been there. Frustration, boredom and a range of negative emotional affects follow from this lack of information to the waiting public. A final, but not trivial, consideration in planning for better queue management according to Pearce (1989) relates to the physical needs of people who are standing in line. There is a need to provide shelter from the sun or rain, a need to provide resting opportunities, drinking fountains, and possibly the scope for a passout card or access to toilet facilities in the longer queues. Additionally, it is said to be desirable that family members can stand side by side in the queue since this facilitates conversation compared to a strict linear queue arrangement. Queue 'width' is also said to be important for children who benefit from a wider queue by having more room to stretch, interact and relate to their care-givers than is possible in confined, one-person wide corridors.

Pearce holds that these psychological and physical needs of people in queues can be met with a range of innovative queue management techniques. These include detailed attention to the shape of the queue. Outside queues which follow form 5 can be easily provided with shade/shelter protection by adding to the exterior of the relevant building. In conclusion, Pearce holds that the attraction starts the moment one joins the queue, rather than the queue simply being a dull preliminary to the main event. Pearce (1989) has made a number of recommendations for queue organisation in relation to specific tourist settings. The matrix proposed by Pearce makes suggestions for eight tourist queue settings. These recommendations are based on principles related to the mental and physical needs of those waiting in line. The recommendations are said not be definitive since the size of the queues, the space of the particular facility and cost factors in personnel may prevent some choices being made. Nevertheless, the matrix is provided in order to challenge and stimulate thinking about future queue management in tourist settings.

For transport service (taxis, bus stops) and small restaurants there commended queue type is said to be the single line with one serviceperson. This queue type is said to be serviceable when the waiting lines are fast moving and space for other queue forms is limited. Pearce finds that in many situations, providing direct information on the service to be used (e.g. cab hire fees, restaurant menus), as well as for general contextual information such as regional attractions would add to the visitor experience. Queue width (at least 2 m) and leaning rails are helpful in transport services where passengers have luggage and are likely to be in small groups. The single line with multiple service personnel queue type is recommended for longer queues where space is constructed into tunnels, hallways and corridors. Pearce believes that much can and should be done in these settings to relieve consumer frustration and boredom by employing information (wait times, entertainment, e.g. videos, and precise instructions) and physical comfort options (seats, moving platforms, toilets).

A better queue type for most large open spaces found in airports as well as in food and customs/immigration facilities is said to be the multiple lines, multiple service personnel system. Here visitors regain some sense of psychological control by being able to see the end of the queue, the speed of processing of the queue and, if information is well organised, their choices and options at the service point. Where such queues are likely to be slow moving, seating and physical facilities options, e.g. leaning rails and water fountains, in the queue can add interest and facilitate visitor comfort. Pearce believes that designers working on the layout of queue facilities should be guided by Fraisse's maxim that it is 'not paying attention to time which makes it pass quickly'. Consequently, the queue shape and associated facilities should aim to mentally stimulate and physically relax its participants. Multiple lines with single service personnel can be recommended for less intense use periods in such situations as theatre or film ticket purchase and food service counters. Pearce believes that while the multiple service personnel option is still preferable in these settings, management costs may prevent using multiple staff. Nevertheless, the multiple lines queue will usually be better for the customer than the single line queue since more individuals in the queue can visually monitor the service point, they can see more of the service/attraction and they can better share any information/entertainment services provided than would be possible in a single queue. The potential sociability of such queues is said to be much greater than for the single line queue type.

One of the strongest recommendations on waiting-in-line situations which emerges from Pearce's discussion is the considerable advantage of using themed queues. In most situations where space is adequate it is recommended that queues be built into the structure of facilities such as large restaurants, theme park entrances, rides and cultural attractions (such as heritage buildings and art galleries). By specifically designing the queue as a part of the fabric of the attraction the visitor experience begins on arrival at the destination. Pearce points out that much can be achieved with awnings, verandahs, rails, seats, interpretive signs and games in the theming process. In larger settings, the 'take a ticket' numbering system can free people from the queuing process which further permits an entrance space to become a room or exhibit area with full physical comfort facilities. In summary, Pearce reports that queues do not have to be a bleak introduction to a tourist attraction. Instead he argues that they can be integrated into the design of a facility, they can provide an opportunity to orientate people towards that facility with questions and display panels, and they can be less onerous physically with the provision of resting opportunities, occasional seats, water fountains, and indicators of time. In some settings Pearce believes that it is possible to provide videos as information sources to the waiting public while in others live entertainment can engage the minds of the audience. Finally, Pearce makes the point that the critical issue to be addressed at tourist attractions is the need to attend to the visitor at all times and people in queues should not be exempt from this attentive service.

Communication processes and environmental interpretation

A fundamentally important aspect of environmental interpretation is effective communication. Ryan and Dewar (1995) have investigated communication processes at Louisbourg National Historic Park, Nova Scotia. The park contains, as one of its main features, a reproduction of an 18th-century wooden fort of the period of French exploration of North America. It receives over 150,000 visits per annum from, it is estimated, 140,000 visitors. In the first stage of their study a modified Communication Competency Scale was used to rank four interpreters working in the kitchen environment; and to rank four interpreters taking visitors on guided walks. The second stage of this study was to test visitors for recall information provided by the interpreters. The evaluation of the interpreters was undertaken by two senior supervisory staff using a modified Communication Competency Scale. Both of the supervisors were reported to have over five years' experience. Twenty-eight evaluations were completed. The volunteer interpreters were not aware of the content of the scale, but had been told the results would be discussed with them when the tests were finished.

Ryan and Dewar conclude that their results offer evidence for the measurement of communication competency in a 'practical' heritage setting by the use of a slightly modified communication competency scale. They further support its usefulness as a training and monitoring tool. Some evidence is provided to support the contention that such scales can be used to measure communication skills. They also argue that evidence is provided of learning by visitors to the national park: learning which has been retained for a period of up to six months. They maintain that this study confirms previous work such as that of Ryan (1990) in that educative/interpretive initiatives can produce retained additional learning for periods of several months after the visit. Finally, these findings also add to the debate about linkages between enjoyment and learning.

Legitimacy in ecotourism

Lawrence, Wickins and Phillips (1997) have examined a number of issues associated with notions of legitimacy as they may affect ecotourism. It is pointed out that, while ecotourism is often recognised for its economic growth potential and source of employment for many communities, it must grapple with a number of looming problems. They believe that a crisis of legitimacy has developed, arising basically out of the various and often conflicting expectations and goals of stakeholders in ecotourism. A fundamental problem here is said to be the lack of institutional standards for ecotourism practice and performance.

Lawrence *et al.* hold that the future success of the ecotourism industry will turn on the successful management of legitimacy at three levels: the firm level, the organisational field level and the industry level. At the firm level, individual companies are urged to develop skills necessary to deal expeditiously with issues as they present themselves. Lawrence *et al.* urge ecotourism operators to attempt to anticipate the types of responses that their activities are likely to provoke in the wider community. The battle to enhance or diminish perceptions of legitimacy is said likely to take place at this stage. They hold that considerable barriers to successful development of ecotourism products are likely to remain when legitimacy perceptions are not considered important or attended to. They point out that the literature on public issues management, in particular legitimacy management, do provide insights for firms into the ways organisations can diminish the probability of facing such damaging legitimacy crises, and also effective management and containment of such a crisis if one was to occur.

A central part of the solution, Lawrence *et al.* maintain, lies in the development and then the communication of standards for ecotourism practice. This is seen necessary at both the organisational field level (sub-industry grouping such as mountaineering or cultural tours) and at the industry level. They make the point that government regulation, industry association activity and collaboration among ecotourism companies must all be directed at the establishment of standards of ecotourism practice. An active industry association is seen as helpful in providing a context for managing stakeholders' concerns. As well, organisational field associations are said to be useful in establishing norms of behaviour against which legitimacy judgements can be made by individual ecotourism operators. Industry associations, Lawrence *et al.* believe, ought to provide public relations and marketing advice which would be likely to reduce the possibility of a legitimacy problem along with the financial and reputational damage a firm and possibility the industry might sustain.

Lawrence *et al.* argue that ecotourism stakeholders should successfully manage this problem of legitimacy. This will involve an effective accommodation of the two central imperatives of the ecotourism industry: economic and ecological. They call for a recognition that all stakeholders inevitably bring with them their own definitions of economic development and also ecological consideration, and how this ideally ought to be balanced. Finally, they make the point that a constructive synthesis of these perspectives which produces effective legitimacy management will involve a process that is founded upon open communication and unhurried collaboration.

Summary

This chapter has provided an understanding of the role and importance of environmental factors in the comprehension of tourist behaviour. The chapter has presented material on topics such as environmental images, cognitive maps, and queuing behaviour. This chapter has also examined the communication process in environmental interpretation as well as issues associated with legitimacy management within an ecotourism context.

CHAPTER 4 DISCUSSION TOPICS

Describe factors which are said to facilitate the development of tourist cognitive maps.

How may mental images be analysed?

Describe various types of tourist queues.

Identify the queue management techniques that reduce visitor dissatisfaction.

Describe legitimacy issues involved in ecotourism at the firm level.

SECTION 2

The Societal and Organisational Contexts of Tourism

6
Tourist Destination Images

LEARNING OBJECTIVES

An understanding of:

- The dimensions of destination image.
- The current research context of backpacker or budget travellers in regard to destination image and evaluation.
- The role of awareness and familiarity in destination choice.
- Pictorial roles in destination image.

This chapter will provide an examination of destination images within the tourism marketing arena. The chapter will cover topics such as image formation, image dimensions and methodological issues. The chapter will then provide case studies focusing on research projects which have explored these topics within various international contexts.

The value of images

National images have, over the last few decades, received considerable research scrutiny (see Min Han 1989). Elements of the tourist industry spend large sums of money attempting to build an image for their destination. The diverse media images of various Australian Barrier Reef islands such as Lizard, Hamilton and Great Keppel are examples of this. Crompton (1979a) has defined vacation destination images as 'the sum of beliefs, ideas and impressions that a person has of a destination' (p. 18). In recent years, more attention has been paid by researchers with a behavioural science background to the form and function of images in the tourist's destination selection process (e.g. Pearce 1988). Hunt (1975) has made the point that images of destination may have as much as, or more, to do with an area's tourist image projection than the more tangible recreation resources. Indeed campaigns by Paul Hogan in the United States to develop an image of Australia as a friendly, attractive and environmentally diverse tourist destination in the estimation of Americans appear to have been more successful in generating interest and Australia-bound travel than previous campaigns based more on the circulation of factual information. Thus image would seem to be much more important in this context than might appear to be the case at first thought.

Dimensions of destination image

Mayo (1975), investigating the basic components of destination image within the leisure context, argues that there are three basic dimensions or important attributes of holiday destinations in the minds of United States tourists: scenery, congestion and climate. Mayo holds that the ideal destination for most tourists would offer a great deal of scenery; it would not be congested either with people or industry, though neither would it be sparsely populated. As well, the ideal destination, according to Mayo, would offer a very comfortable climate. Finally, Mayo notes that 'in terms of scenery, congestion and climate, the National Parks (in the United States) enjoy a very strong image' (1975: 15). These findings are generally supported by the work of Anderssen and Colberg (1973) who concluded that the dominant attributes are cost, climate and scenery.

Hunt (1975) has suggested that distance from a region may be an important ingredient in image formation. In a study of a four-state tourist region of the Rocky Mountains, Hunt found respondents who resided further from this region did not differentiate areas within the region as well as those respondents from closer areas. Images of holiday destinations also seem to change over time and as the result of experience. Gartner (1986) has found that the image of a region, in this instance Utah in the US, demonstrated some perceptual change even over a short-term period. He argues that much research has yet to be done in this area, particularly in the area of perceptual change over time in regard to destination image. Pearce (1982) has found that perceptual change also takes place after experiencing various destinations. He has found evidence that tourists visiting destinations such as Greece and Morocco underwent a change of image as a result of the visit. Thus actual experience of a destination would seem to alter the image of this destination held by the visitor.

Crompton (1979a), in a study of the image of Mexico as a potential vacation destination for US residents, found that ideal holiday destination images and actual images of Mexico differed considerably. Negative image attributes to emerge from a comparison of Mexico's actual and ideal destination image related primarily to sanitation and safety, whereas more positive attributes related to climate and low cost. Crompton also reported that the further away respondents resided from Mexico, the more favourable were their images of that country as a vacation destination. Crompton concluded that the greater the gap between actual and ideal images, the less likelihood there is that an individual will opt to visit this destination. Hoffman and Low (1978), in a study of visitors to Phoenix, Arizona, found that the most important variable in any decision to return in the future was the visitor's image of the friendliness of the residents. Thus the decision to return was not so much influenced by images of the area's facilities and attributes nor visitor's place of origin or distance from origin, but by the friendliness of the local population in the estimation of the visitor.

Methodological issues

Echtner and Ritchie (1991) have pointed out that there are a wide variety of methodologies employed in destination image studies. Echtner and Ritchie also make the point that many researchers evidence a liking for structured methodologies and typically employ Likert Scales or the Semantic Differential. They go on to make the point that these methodological preferences, by their nature, tend to preclude more holistic perspectives as well as unique components associated with particular destinations. Echtner and Ritchie argue that researchers ought not rely so heavily upon secondary surveys in order to compile the research internment, but rather focus more attention on the initial stage of scale compilation, and employ techniques such as focus groups in order to access a more complete range of destination images among visitors. Finally, Echtner and Ritchie (1991) point out that present methodologies often fail to capture the psychological dimension within destination image research. They point out that the only psychological characteristic measured by many is friendliness. While functional measures are recognised as important, they believe that a greater attention paid to the initial stages of destination research and the use of qualitative procedures such as focus groups will result in a more valid and reliable instrument.

Destination evaluation and the backpacker segment

Pearce (1990c) has made the point that the budget traveller may best be defined in social rather than economic or demographic terms. He offered a number of basic criteria by which this type of traveller may be identified. Those criteria include a preference for budget accommodation, an emphasis on meeting other travellers, an independently arranged and flexible travel plan, longer vacations and a preference for informal, unstructured vacation activities.

Pearce goes on to make the point that these individuals tend to be under 40 years of age and include travellers from the host country as well as from other countries. Some commentators have also argued that the budget traveller is not a recent phenomenon in the history of travel. Riley (1988) described how many commentators regard tourism as originating, in major part, from the grand tour taken by young European aristocrats in the seventeenth and eighteenth centuries. Riley points out that the grand tour had equivalents in the long-term religious and labour-related travel of the lower classes of Europe of this period. This form of tourism she styles as 'tramping', and argues that it afforded opportunities for adventure, sightseeing and general education by way of hands-on experience. Thus the young workingman's equivalent to the 'grand tour' is said to be a precursor to the present day phenomenon of budget travelling, or backpacking.

There are both theoretical and methodological deficiencies apparent in many tourism evaluation studies in such contexts. Visitor profiles have traditionally been the favoured aim for many proprietors of a recreational area or destination who want to know more about the people who use their facility or destination. However, visitor reactions are increasingly seen as important, for they primarily reflect tourists' cognitions, satisfactions and emotional reactions to a specific tourist venue (Ross 1989a, 1990c). Pearce and Moscardo (1984) have examined the research evidence associated with visitor venues in various contexts and locations. In this regard they cite the research of the Countryside Commission (1979) in the United Kingdom. This study utilised a psychological framework in its assessment of visitor centres, and recognised that the central product offered by any tourist location is the experience, a point also emphasised by commentators such as Iso-Ahola (1980). The Countryside Commission looked at factors such as visitor enjoyment and motivation, and related these factors to both environmental variables and visitor demographics. It was concluded from this study, and also emphasised by Pearce and Moscardo (1984), that psychological factors such as perceived enjoyment are powerful predictors in any evaluation of a tourist venue or destination.

There is also generally a dearth of empirical research in regard to particular destination evaluations by market segments such as budget travellers. There is, however, now a growing literature on topics such as budget travellers' roles and motivation (e.g. Pearce 1982c, 1988, 1990c; Cohen 1973, 1982) as well as basic elements of the road culture of budget travellers (e.g. Mukerji 1978; Riley 1988). Riley has made the point that budget travellers are individuals who basically have extended their travels beyond that of the cyclical holiday. She argues that their motives relate both to push and pull factors. They are said to be escaping from the orderliness and predictability of their daily lives and often routine employment. They are further said to be, in many instances, temporarily escaping from the long-term commitments associated with marriage and family. These individuals are thus seen to be at major decision-points of life, either having a last great adventure before the long-term demands of family and career encompass them, or escaping from boredom or even dissatisfaction with work or a close relationship.

Riley also described some of the pull factors that budget travellers are said to experience. She argues that while the choice to experience a greater sense of freedom in destinations regarded as much more exotic than home is a powerful determinant for many, the simple desire to learn by long-term travel is also an important factor in the decision-making processes of many budget travellers. She makes the point that ego enhancement by way of both knowledge acquisition and the deepening of philosophical understanding is a likely cause of travel for many in this group. Graburn (1983) has written of 'rite-of-passage' tourism. He has argued that such a traveller is typically in the process of undergoing major life transitions. A person in this group may be in the process of becoming an adult, severing unsatisfying relationships, or attempting to solve or reverse apparently intractable personal or work problems. Graburn makes the point that this type of traveller is typically long-term and interested in self-development. Riley (1988) has made the point the Graburn's typology accurately fits the budget traveller.

Pearce (1990a) has pointed out that the budget traveller phenomenon did not emerge in Australia as early as it did in Europe and Asia. Cohen (1973) has written of the 'drifter' traveller who prefers to stray from the beaten track and avoid the more conventional tourist establishments. Such individuals were described as predominantly coming from a middle-class context and seeking enriching and novel life experiences within totally different and exciting destinations. Pearce has pointed out that by the 1970s the 'drifter' had become the 'hippie' traveller. Moreover, much greater proportions of such travellers were now female and had originated from working-class families. By the 1980s Australian destinations such as Cairns and the Wet Tropics region of Northern Australia had become well known and heavily patronised by many budget travellers. Pearce (1990a) made the point that the 'core' trip for budget travellers to Australia is typically Sydney-Cairns, with over 90% of a sample from a major Australian study reporting such a preferred and likely travel pattern. Thus by the 1980s cities such as Cairns had come to be regarded as a major destination for most of this segment who visit Australia.

Wet tropics destination images

This section will explore concepts and issues relevant within the ecotourism context. The destination chosen is the Wet Tropics World Heritage Area of Northern Australia. This destination has seen a major influx of tourists since the Australian Bicentenary in 1988, and now receives a large and growing number of visitors, both from southern Australia and from overseas. Zube (1976) has argued that physical environments can be placed on a continuum ranging from the most natural through various stages to the almost totally constructed landscape. The tropical rainforests of Northern Queensland have recently received a great deal of publicity in the Australian media. Within this publicity the wet tropics are effectively portrayed as being at one end of Zube's continuum, a wilderness area, a diverse collection of landforms, biological and cultural phenomena which has remained relatively pristine and unaltered by humans in recent times. However, it may be that not every person regards the rainforests of north Queensland in such a manner or is attracted to this type of destination. Some people, whether they be interstate/overseas tourists or local residents, may hold a different constellation of images about the wet tropics of Australia, and may have ideal holiday destination images very different to these.

This study by Ross (1991) aimed to derive an ideal holiday destination image profile as well as an actual profile of the wet tropics of Far North Queensland from a sample of tourists visiting this region. The study aimed to investigate divergences between ideal and actual images using a profile of destination attributes employed in previous studies such as those of Crompton (1979c) and Mayo (1975). Studies such as those of Crompton have concentrated on negative divergences where actual destination images such as sanitation fall short of the ideal. This study focused on the hitherto uninvestigated domain of positive divergences where actual images such as destination resident friendliness may exceed the ideal. It was hypothesised that the attributes of climate, congestion and scenery would also be prominent within the derived profiles, and that a positive divergence between ideal and actual images of the friendliness of local residents would affect the estimations of the holiday destination and the decision to return in the future.

The data in Table 6.1 reveal significant differences between eight actual and ideal images. The wet tropics were more likely to be associated with bad roads, expensive souvenirs, expensive public transport, crowded resorts, wet winters, and also were more likely to possess uncrowded roads, friendly locals and exotic wildlife. Other attributes of the Australian wet tropics appeared to match visitors' images of an ideal holiday destination.

This study explored aspects of the relationships between tourists' ideal holiday images and actual images of the wet tropics of Far North Queensland. For most of the destination attributes around which images were formed there appeared to be a close correspondence between the ideal and the actual. Thus for many visitors to this tourist destination the ideal and actual images included relatively higher ratings on attributes such as authenticity, a varied physical environment and exotic landscapes, and neutral ratings on attributes such as educated residents, safe environmental contexts, and winter temperature. However, for a number of destination images there was a negative divergence between the actual and the ideal. Visitors saw the roads, the cost of souvenirs and public transport and the larger number of people at tourist resorts as less than their ideal. The negative images appear to focus on aspects of the constructed environment rather than natural environment. It may be that aspects of the built environment in this context were judged as inferior or inadequate when compared with the quality of those in larger urban centres such as New York or Tokyo. Alternatively, it may be that a comparison process is activated, whereby aspects of the built environment come to be regarded as out of place and detracting from the beauty of the rainforest environment. In this way these attributes may accrue a negative image around themselves. Visitors regarded the uncrowded roads, the friendly locals and the exotic wildlife as surpassing their ideals in a tourist destination. The outstanding positive images associated with the Australian wet tropics focus on a lack of congestion on the roadways, outstanding scenery involving remarkable or unusual wildlife, and images of the locals as friendlier than is normally required to judge a destination as ideal.

While factors such as scenery and congestion have been highlighted in previous destination image studies (Crompton 1979b in the US; Ross 1988 in Kakadu), relatively little attention has been paid to the potency of images of destination residents in the decision-making processes of tourists. In one study Hoffman and Low (1978) found that the factor most responsible for increasing the likelihood of a tourist expressing a desire to return to a destination is his/her estimation of the friendliness of the local residents. Ross (1991a) has revealed that those tourists whose ideal image includes friendly locals are also more likely to see the residents of this destination as friendly and are more likely to express an intention to return, while the tourists whose ideal image is neutral here are also more likely to see the locals as neither friendly nor unfriendly and are less likely to be associated with actual neutral images. Thus ideal and actual images occurred in both friendly and neutral categories, but not unfriendly categories. There are relatively few visitors with ideal or actual negative images. Visitors to this destination appear to be predominantly friendly or neutral in their ideal image of local residents, and to mirror this in actual images.

Most visitors rated the wet tropics of Australia highly as a holiday destination. Those whose actual image was friendly were more likely to rate this destination as excellent. Those whose ideal was neutral were less likely to rate it as excellent, and those whose ideal was friendly were less likely to rate the wet tropics as a neutral holiday destination. Once again categories involving unfriendly ideal images or unsuitable ratings appeared to be relatively

Table 6.1 Wet Tropics destination images, ideal holiday destination images, and mean differences for destination attributes, with paired t values and probability levels

Destination Image	M Wet	M Ideal	M WT-I	Paired t-value	Prob. (2 tail)
Roads (Good-Bad)	2.941	2.5	.441	4.568	.0001
Landscapes (Exotic-Ordinary)	2.667	2.74	−.074		
Environment (Unsafe-Safe)	3.088	3.26	−.172		
Residents (Educated-Uneduc.)	2.922	2.985	−.064		
Souvenirs (Expensive-Inexpensive)	2.77	3.029	−.26	−2.83	.005
Roads (Crowded-Uncrowded)	2.632	2.838	−.206	−1.97	.05
Public transport (Expensive-inexpensive)	2.951	3.328	−.377	−3.499	.001
Resorts (Uncrowded-Crowded)	2.819	2.593	.25	2.42	.02
Summers (Hot-Mild)	2.593	2.75	−.157		
Summers (Wet-Dry)	2.789	2.936	−.147		
Winters (Dry-Wet)	3.402	2.917	.485	4.49	.001
Winters (Cold-Mild)	3.015	3.167	−.152		
Physical environment (Varied-Uniform)	2.657	2.564	.093		
Locals (Friendly-Unfriendly)	2.672	2.495	.176	2.05	.05
Wildlife (Familiar-Exotic)	2.559	2.343	.216	2.4	.02
Environment (Authentic-Artificial)	2.309	2.235	.074		

Source: Ross, 1991a

unimportant. There is further evidence here of a matching between an ideal image of friendly locals and ratings of the wet tropics as a holiday destination, and little likelihood that high ratings on one variable were likely to produce neutral ratings on another. This pattern was also evident, though to a lesser extent, for the congestion and wildlife images.

Visitors generally expressed an intention to return to this destination at some time in the future. Those more likely to do so had a friendly or somewhat friendly image of the residents of the wet tropics, confirming the findings of Hoffman and Low (1978) in Arizona. Those less likely to do so enjoyed a neutral but not unfriendly image. In this instance the match principally involves the somewhat friendly and the neutral images. Again unfriendly images generally appear to be absent from this sample, giving rise to the suggestion that such individuals are either absent or experience a shift of image. It is worth noting here that the decision to return to this destination might also be influenced by factors such as finance, distance or a desire for vacation diversity.

This study produced both ideal and actual image profiles, and highlighted the finding that the major destination attributes positively divergent from the ideal involve congestion, scenery and local residents. Images of local residents emerged as an important explanatory variable, with a matching process in evidence between equivalent levels of actual and ideal images, between actual images and destination ratings, and between actual images and reported intention to return. It would thus seem that tourists with ideal images differing from the actual are less likely to find themselves at a destination such as this. It may be that visitors only travel to a destination if the specific image of the residents is matched with the ideal image, or it may be that a matching process occurs at some point during the visit.

Awareness and familiarity in destination choice

Milman and Pizam (1995) have conducted a study based on theoretical notions regarding the consumer's buying process incorporating product awareness, familiarity, interest, and purchase. A series of hypotheses were tested to analyse whether consumer awareness and familiarity with Central Florida as a vacation destination had an impact on the consumer's destination image and on the interest and likelihood to visit it. Their results indicated that those who were familiar with Central Florida (i.e. had previously visited it) had a more positive image of the destination and were more interested and likely to revisit it than those who were aware of the destination. Their findings suggest that familiarity with the destination (i.e. previous visitation) had a significant impact on future intentions and, therefore, may forward the consumer into a more advanced stage in the purchasing decision process (i.e. repeat visitation). With regard to the impact of awareness, contrary to their expectations respondents who were aware of Central Florida as a vacation destination did not have a more positive image of Central Florida than those who were not aware of it. The same they found to be true in the case of interest in and likelihood to visit Central Florida. Those respondents who were aware of the destination (but did not visit it) did not necessarily express a greater interest and/or likelihood to visit it.

Their results point out a significant improvement in the image of the destination and an increase in the interest in and likelihood of visiting it when consumers go from the awareness to the familiarity stage. However, the evidence presented in their study fails to show a similar increase occurring when consumers move from the non-awareness to the awareness stage. The results, they believe, seem to support Fesenmaier, Vogt, and Stewart's (1993) study and indicate that awareness may not always lead to an interest in the destination or intent to visit it. Milman and Pizam conclude that awareness results, at best, in curiosity that can lead to interest and eventually to trial.

Pictorial roles in destination images

The role of pictorial elements in the formation of destination image has been subjected to increasing scrutiny. McKay and Fesenmaier (1997) have sought to investigate aspects of the promoted and perceived image of destinations. They note that there are identifiable processes and factors which mediate the degree of overlap between promoted and perceived images, and hold that an understanding of the sources of variation is important in the conceptualisation of both image formation theory and image marketing efforts. McKay and Fesenmaier point out that differences in interpretation of visuals can be attributed to differences in the pictures being evaluated, differences among the individuals performing the evaluation, as well as interactions between these two factors. In an assessment of previous literature on the subject they conclude that both personal factors (such as demographics, culture and familiarity) and also attributes of the object being perceived (such as physical features) have been found pertinent to an understanding of image assessment. McKay and Fesenmaier have sought to extend understandings of the relationship between promotional and perceived images, making the point that an imaginary perspective is a useful tool in the comprehension of the effects of tourism advertising. They clearly point out that pictures not only present the touristic product, but also in many instances communicate attributes, characteristics, concepts, values and ideas to tourists and potential tourists.

McKay and Fesenmaier have sought to investigate the manner by which visuals conveying symbolic, experiential and also structural aspects of a national park influenced the way destination image is created, viewed, interpreted and finally evaluated. They have concluded that the concept of destination image is tri-dimensional, with image dimensions generated from visual aspects (i.e. attractiveness, uniqueness and texture). Moreover, the image dimensions so formed were said to convey the underlying dimensional structure of tourism destination image, namely psychological-functional, common-unique and attribute-holistic. McKay and Fesenmaier report that in many cases, dimensions of the visual were found to be the most significant predictors of destination image. They concluded that individuals were taking their image of a particular destination from the visual dimensions, namely attractiveness, uniqueness and texture. Finally, they make the point that destination image formation was a composite of both individual inputs and also marketer inputs.

Summary

This chapter has provided a coverage of a number of major topics within the marketing of tourist destinations from the standpoint of disciplines such as psychology. Major issues covered have included image formation and image dimensions as well as methodological issues associated with competent research in this context. Also examined was a recent ecotourism study in the Wet Tropics Region of Northern Australia, which has explored these issues and notions. This study has revealed distinctive images and touristic mental processes which provide opportunities for further ecotourism research. The chapter concludes with an examination of results from recent studies which have investigated the roles of awareness and familiarity in the determination of vacation destination and pictorial roles in destination images.

CHAPTER 6 DISCUSSION TOPICS

Describe some major dimensions of destination image.

What were the historical antecedents of the backpacker?

Outline major aspects of the role of the present day backpacker in an ecotourism context.

What role does awareness play in destination choice?

Outline the visual dimension of destination image formation.

7

Human Resource Management and the Tourism/ Hospitality Industry

LEARNING OBJECTIVES

An understanding of:

- The mechanisms of work motivation.
- The role of values and their expression within work satisfaction.
- The importance of expectancies in energising work.
- The role of needs theory as applied to tourism/hospitality employment.
- Anglo-Greek tourism career perceptions.

Work for many people assumes a far greater importance than simply earning a living or survival. This chapter will examine some of the major theories of motivation within psychology as they attempt to explain why it is that people want to work. It will do this by reference to theorists such as Maslow, McClelland, Rokeach, Feather, and Porter and Lawler, elaborating on a number of major areas as the hierarchy of needs within the Maslow tradition, the needs-press theories within the Murray/McClelland tradition, and the value/expectancy theories within the Rokeach/Feather tradition. It is argued that such theoretical formulations hold considerable promise in their ability to comprehend work behaviour within the tourism/ hospitality industry. The chapter will then examine recent studies which focus on some of these concepts as they are applied to tourism/hospitality industry employment.

Motivation to work

Perhaps one of the most widely known and accepted psychological approaches for understanding why people work or desire to is Maslow's (1970) straightforward yet comprehensive schema of human needs. The five levels of need in this schema can be used as neat conceptual categories for grouping together the various studies and theories that have proliferated in recent years in attempts to explain why individuals work. The following is a basic outline of Maslow's schema applied to work motivation.

Maslow's lowest two levels of needs, those relating to biological survival, can be linked to work motives for income, prospects, security and safety:

• the need for an income at least sufficient to maintain a basic level of existence.
• the need for prospects such as the possibility of increasing income; there is a societal expectancy that people's efforts will bring in greater returns as they age, at least until retirement.
• the need for security for an ongoing income.
• the need for safety; adequate standards of health and safety, hours of work, working conditions and medical care.

It is generally the case that while early management theories saw people as basically motivated by money, the majority of studies have now concluded that money is neither the only, nor the predominant factor. Stagner (1950) in an extensive study of employees' motivations asked what was most important to them at work. Stagner found that only 7% gave rates of pay as most important whereas 36% gave a steady job as their predominant value. Perhaps the study that has had most impact here was that completed by Morse and Weiss (1955) who interviewed a nationwide US sample as to whether they would give up work if they inherited enough money to live comfortably without working. They found that over 80% indicated that they would keep on working. However, not all the evidence points in this direction. Goldthorpe, Lockwood, Bechofer and Platt (1968), sampling manual workers at an age when they were likely to have the greatest financial responsibilities, found that the majority indicated that they worked primarily for money in order to maintain a standard of living and to gain material possessions. Work, to these people, was simply a means to an end. They did not expect to gain satisfaction from what they were doing at work or from those with whom they associated at work. Thus research has found differences among social classes in the strength of economic motivation. In this regard, the more skilled employees are more likely to be motivated by non-economic factors.

Maslow's third level of need is affiliation. Social isolation is one of the main reasons given by many people such as mothers for returning to work. It has long been known that one of the most common ways that groups have of punishing members who fail to conform to group norms is to 'send them to Coventry', that is to keep them isolated. Commentators believe that the Hawthorne experiment did much to highlight the social motive for work, and while some doubts have since been expressed as to whether this was so central a motive as Mayo argued at the time, there is nonetheless a truth remaining in it (Roethlisberger and Dickson 1939). These studies, carried out at the Hawthorne works of the Western Electric Company in Chicago, set out to examine the effects of lighting conditions on output and later to examine other changes in working conditions, such as hours of work and methods of payment. Eventually the researchers were forced to conclude that what seemed to have most effect involved being taken notice of and working in a co-operative team. While their research methodology has subsequently received some criticism, many would still agree with the general conclusions.

Maslow's fourth level of need is for self-esteem. To a significant extent society gives people recognition because of their job. Guidance counsellors and human resource managers frequently encounter clients who choose certain alternatives, not because the work really interests them or because they have the abilities for it, but because it has a certain image, and that is the image that they want for themselves. To these individuals, what is important is how they want to see themselves and how they want others to see them.

Maslow's highest level, self-actualisation, is about the motive to experience challenges and to develop as a person. People here are said to seek work which will allow them to develop their self-image, to expand, and to harness their potential as fully as possible. The Hawthorne experiments questioned the economic motive as being a sufficient explanation of why people work. Herzburg's studies (Herzburg, Mausner and Snyderman 1959), may be seen as lending support to Maslow's (1970) concepts of higher levels of motivations. Herzburg asked people to describe occasions when they found themselves satisfied at work and occasions when they found themselves dissatisfied. Factors such as money, interpersonal relations, conditions of work and Herzburg's 'hygiene' factors, function as dissatisfiers if they are not adequate, but do not act as positive motivators. Herzburg believed that it was the basic element of the task that serves as the motivator, the satisfier. The elements included in this are the work itself, advancement, achievement, recognition and responsibility. It may be noted that these are the kinds of needs that constitute Maslow's fourth and fifth levels. In conclusion, many commentators now believe that work can provide stimulation and new experiences, and can structure daily life and prevent boredom. For many individuals work can serve to take their minds off their problems and can even prevent other threats such as ill-health due to depression.

Murray's Needs-Press theory

The second needs theory of motivation which has been related to work was developed by Henry A. Murray (1938) and is termed Manifest Needs theory or Needs-Press theory. While the initial formulations were devised by Murray in the 1930s and 1940s, the model has been considerably developed and extended by David McClelland and John Atkinson (Atkinson 1964; McClelland, Atkinson, Clark and Lowell 1953). Like Maslow, Murray believed that individuals could be classified according to the strengths of various needs. People were thought to possess at any one time a variety of divergent (and sometimes conflicting) needs which influence behaviour. A need here was defined as a 'recurrent concern for a goal state' (McClelland 1971). Each need was said to be made up of two components:

1   A qualitative, or directional component which includes the object towards which the need is directed; and
2   A quantitative, or energetic component which consists of the strength or intensity of the need towards the object.

Needs were thus viewed as the central motivating force for people in terms of both direction and intensity. Murray posited that individuals possess approximately two dozen needs, including the needs for achievement, affiliation, power and autonomy. Murray believed that needs are mostly learned, rather than inherited, and are activated (or manifested) by cues from the external environment. For example, an employee who had a high need for achievement would only be expected to pursue that need (i.e. try to achieve a specific work goal) when the environmental conditions were appropriate (i.e. when the worker was given a challenging task). Only then would the need become manifest. When the need was not met, the need was said to be latent or not activated.

The most prominent and well known need from the standpoint of understanding behaviour in the workplace is the need for achievement (also known as n Ach or n Achievement). Need for achievement is defined as 'behaviour toward competition with a standard of excellence' (McClelland et al. 1953). High need for achievement is characterised by:

1   A strong desire to assume personal responsibility for finding solutions to problems;
2   A tendency to set moderately difficult achievement goals and take calculated risks;
3   A strong desire for concrete feedback on task performance; and
4   A single-minded preoccupation with task and task accomplishment.

Low need for achievement is typically characterised by a preference for low risk levels on tasks and for shared responsibility on tasks.

The concept of need for achievement is said to be important for understanding how people respond to the work environment. Enriching an employee's job by providing greater amounts of variety, autonomy and responsibility would probably enhance performance only for those individuals who were challenged by such a job (i.e. high need achievers). Low need achievers, on the other hand, may be frustrated by the increased personal responsibility for task accomplishment and may perform poorly or even attempt to leave the situation.

The need for affiliation (n Aff) focuses on the individual worker's need for relationships with other people. The need for affiliation may be defined as an 'attraction to another organism in order to feel reassured from the other that the self is acceptable' (Birch and Veroff 1966:65). This need is not to be equated with being sociable or popular, but rather is the need for human companionship and reassurance. People with a high need for affiliation are typified by the following:

1   A strong desire for approval and reassurance from others;
2   A tendency to conform to the wishes and norms of others when pressured by people whose friendship they value; and
3   A sincere interest in the feelings of others.

High n Aff individuals are said to seek jobs characterised by a high amount of interpersonal contact, like sales, teaching, public relations and counselling.

The third major need in McClelland's schema is that for autonomy (n Aut). This need is said to be a desire for independence and for freedom from any kind of constraint. Individuals with a high need for autonomy prefer situations where they:

1   Work alone;
2   Control their own pace;
3   Are not hampered by excessive rules or procedures governing their work behaviour (Birch and Veroff 1966).

Birch and Veroff argue that the effects of a high n Aut on employee behaviour can be significant. It has been found that high n Aut individuals tend not to react to external pressure for conformity to group norms (Kasl, Sampson and French 1964), tend to be poor performers unless they are allowed to participate in the determination of their work tasks (Vroom 1959), tend not to be committed to the goals of the organisation, and generally do not aspire to become managers (Vroom 1959). This last finding, it is said, may be explained by the fact that managerial success is in large measure determined by a manager's ability to interact successfully with others, to co-operate and to compromise. Individuals with a high n Aut are said to typically decline to do this.

A final need that has been said to be important for the understanding of behaviour in work situations is an individual's need for power (or dominance). Need for power (n Pow) represents a desire to influence others and to control one's environment. It is said to have a strong social connotation, in contrast to n Aut, in that a high n Pow employee will try to control or lead those around him/her. Interest in the power motive is said to date from the work of Alfred Adler in the 1930s who believed that power was the major goal of all human activity. While the work of Murray and McClelland does not see power as an all-consuming drive as Adler did, they do view it as an important need, particularly for managers. Those employees with high needs for power and dominance tend to be superior performers, tend to gravitate to supervisory positions, and to be rated by others as having good leadership abilities (see Steers and Braunstein 1976).

Expectancy-valence and employment

The Expectancy-valence theory, or simply Expectancy theory, of work motivation dates from the early work of Kurt Lewin and Edward Tolman during the 1930s and 1940s. These early investigators rejected many of the notions of drive theory and instead argued that much of human behaviour results from interaction between the characteristics of individuals (e.g. their personality traits, attitudes, needs and values), and their environment. This basic model was first applied to work settings by Georgopoulus, Mahoney, and Jones (1957) in their path-goal theory of motivation. It is worth noting that expectancy theory is known by various titles, including path-goal theory, instrumental theory, and valence-instrumentality-expectancy theory. According to the basic model, individuals are seen as thinking, reasoning individuals who make conscious choices about present and future behaviour. People are not seen as inherently motivated or unmotivated, as many earlier models suggest. Instead, motivational level is seen as depending on the particular work environment people find themselves in. To the extent that this environment is compatible with their needs, goals and expectations, they are motivated.

The first systematic adumbration of expectancy theory as it relates to work situations was presented by Vroom (1964). This was followed by extensions and refinements on the model by Galbraith and Cummings (1967), Porter and Lawler (1968), Graen (1969) and Campbell et al. (1970). Within expectancy theory, motivation is determined by expectancies and valences. An expectancy is a belief about the likelihood or probability that a particular behavioural act will lead to a particular outcome. Valence refers to the value an individual places on available outcomes or rewards. Lawler (1973) has argued that expectancies can be divided into two types: Effort-Performance expectancies and Performance-Outcome expectancies. An E-P expectancy is an individual's belief that effort will lead to successful performance. Lawler has suggested several influences on the E-P expectancies we form about work. These include level of self-esteem, past experiences in similar situations and perception of the actual situation. A P-O expectancy is the belief that if a person performs well in a given situation certain desired outcomes will follow. Performance-Outcome expectancies are influenced by a variety of factors, including past experience in similar situations, attractiveness of the various outcomes, extent of one's internal locus of control and belief in an ability to control the environment, E-P expectancies, and perception of the actual situation.

Values

Within the last three decades psychology has experienced a remarkable and widespread awareness of the importance of cognitive concepts as potent explanations within the discipline. Social psychology has been at the forefront of this movement, and has rediscovered Lewin's emphasis on the usefulness of intermediate determinants of behaviour (Lewin 1951). One such general cognitive topic is that of the psychology of values. Values within psychology are said to have a reasonably long history, yet are relatively neglected by many social psychologists. The major scale for measuring values has been the Rokeach Value Survey (Rokeach 1973). Rokeach argues that there are two classes of values, terminal and instrumental, and each type is represented in the Rokeach Value Survey (RVS). The terminal values are concerned with general goals or end states of being, and include such values as freedom, equality, self-respect, wisdom and inner harmony. The instrumental values focus on means to goals or styles of conduct. These include such values as being ambitious, courageous, honest, loving, responsible and imaginative. Typically, respondents are requested to rank order each set of values in their order of importance for self as guiding principles for life. This rank order for each set of values provides two value systems for each respondent, a terminal and an instrumental value system. Respondents may then be compared on each of their value systems.

Rokeach's (1973) major conceptual contribution is in his adumbration of a model of the human belief system in which beliefs, attitudes and values are clearly differentiated. Rokeach makes the point that the value construct is applied to a particular type of enduring belief centrally concerned with modes of conduct and end states of being. These are said to transcend specific objects and situations, and for each person are privately and socially preferable to an opposite mode of conduct or end states of existence. Thus the unique characteristics of the value domain are differentiated from those of other beliefs and attitudes.

Values may function to control need-induced behaviour. Yet in other situations a motivational system may have both need and value properties, in that what a person wants to do corresponds with what the person thinks ought to be done. Values are said to have the ability to induce evaluations of good and bad. Both values and needs function as motives in their ability to induce valences, either positive or negative, corresponding to attractive or repulsive regions of the environment. Rokeach (1973) views values as involving the cognitive representation and transformation of needs, and argues that the transformation takes account of societal and institutional demands. Ultimately values are said to be in the service of the self, and they are employed to maintain and enhance self-esteem.

Work values and satisfaction

The relationship between work values and various dimensions of satisfaction has also received growing scrutiny in the last decade or so. In a major Australian study, O'Brien and Dowling (cited by Feather 1979a) investigated specific work values on the assumption that the values most important for understanding how workers react to jobs are those more related to the job itself. They selected five aspects of work which have been found to correspond to formal aspects of the job structure as highlighted by structural role theory (Oeser and O'Brien 1967). These five aspects are:

1 Skill Utilisation (the degree to which there is a match between job skills and the worker's actual skills);
2 Influence (the degree to which the job allows the worker to control or participate in decisions about aspects of job organisation and performance);
3 Variety (the degree to which the job involves different tasks);
4 Pressure (the degree to which task activity is determined by time constraints, machines and other people); and
5 Interaction (the degree to which the job requires and allows contact with other people).

O'Brien and Dowling also used a principle of discrepancy, assuming that a person's overall evaluation of his/her job will depend upon the degree to which actual experiences match or are congruent with desired levels of values for each of the five dimensions. Thus job satisfaction would depend on an interaction between valued job attributes and actual job attributes. Increasing matches between actual job attributes and valued or desired job attributes would be associated with increasing job satisfaction. In this study respondents rated their present jobs on each of these five items, and also responded to the same items so as to provide a measure of desired attributes or work values. In this task respondents were asked to indicate how much of the attribute they would like in their job. As well, a global measure of job satisfaction was also obtained covering different aspects of the job (i.e. supervision, pay, promotion, challenge, etc.). Feather (1979a) reports that their results support the value congruence hypothesis in regard to the dimensions of skill utilisation, influence, variety, but not the other dimensions. O'Brien and Dowling report that the direct effect of desired work attributes and the interactive effect of actual and desired work attributes was relatively small when compared with the effect of actual job attributes, particularly in relation to the dimensions of skill utilisation, variety, and influence. They draw the implication that in order to increase job satisfaction, one should principally increase the amount of skill utilisation, variety and influence within the workplace.

The abovementioned models represent many of the more prominent conceptualisations of work behaviour from the domain of psychology. The next section will present findings from a recent study which explored some of these concepts within a tourism/hospitality industry context.

Personality needs and tourism/hospitality industry employment

Factors mitigating occupational choice among high school students have received relatively little research attention in the organisational/industrial psychology arena, and are often regarded as belonging more to the province of educational or developmental psychology. Thus factors such as specific personality needs and their relationships to vocational choice have been subjected to scant research scrutiny within particular industry/work contexts. The more common focus is on individual and group socio-demographic variables (e.g. Fottler and Bain 1984). In such studies a range of possible occupational choices is examined together with background characteristics of the individual school leaver. In this context it has basically been found that males and individuals from higher socio-economic backgrounds have higher levels of occupational aspiration (Bain and Fottler 1980; Lawrence and Brown 1976). While the mediating role of background variables has thus received some research scrutiny, relatively little work has been done regarding the role of personality variables in occupational choice in regard to emergent industries such as the tourism/hospitality industry. The tourism/hospitality industry is now one of the largest employers in many countries, and a great number of communities look to this industry to provide work opportunities for their school leavers.

Commentators such as Murphy (1985) have found that certain groups of people appear to develop much more positive attitudes towards the tourist industry in any tourism-related community. Residents with a commercial or vocational investment in tourism were more likely to be favourably disposed to the industry than were other community members. Thus those who own or operate businesses, as well as those who work in those businesses, have been found to be more likely to have positive attitudes to the industry than those who have no direct involvement or perceive that they derive no benefit from tourism. Murphy has made the point that familiarity with this industry leads in many instances to more favourable overall evaluations.

Ross (1991a, 1991b) has argued for the utility of specific personality variables in the understanding of vocational choice involving industries such as tourism/hospitality. He has found that variables such as Locus of Control and the Protestant Work Ethic are predictors of career choice in this context, with an internal Locus of Control being associated with more realistic career path perceptions and further education intentions, and the Protestant Work Ethic being associated with an intention to pursue a management career within the tourism/hospitality industry. His study sought to explore McClelland's four major needs as they may predict career aspirations associated with the tourism/hospitality industry or be associated with a set of socio-demographic indicators.

Table 7.1 contains Friedman analysis of variance (by ranks) statistics for the need for Achievement, the need for Autonomy, the need for Dominance and the need for Affiliation. From this table it can be seen that it is the need for Affiliation that has been ranked highest by respondents. The lower scores involved the need for Autonomy and the need for Dominance. The need for Achievement received somewhat more support than did these two, but not to the degree of the need for Affiliation.

The need for Achievement, however, emerged as the most prominent explanatory personality need in this investigation of interest in work in the tourism/hospitality industry, even though it was not rated the highest overall by students. Those individuals with higher levels of need for Achievement were inclined to seek out and associate with people from this prominent local industry who could have influence in the local employment market. It may also be that individuals with a higher need for Achievement are more aware of their friends and acquaintances in this industry because of its economic pre-eminence in the local community. Thus those with higher Achievement needs may have clearer perceptions of the people and the industry most likely to provide them with a future career. Individuals with a higher need for Achievement also demonstrated a higher motivation to work in this particular industry, with a higher expectation of job attainment and also with a preparedness to consider post-secondary school training. Thus students higher in this need were more likely to want to work in this particular industry, believed they had a good chance of attaining their desired employment and were prepared to consider further training to realise this end. It may

Table 7.1 Friedman analysis of variance (by ranks) statistics for the need for Achievement, the need for Autonomy, the need for Dominance and the need for Affiliation.

Variable	S rank	Mean rank
n Ach	1286.5	2.414
n Aut	1168	2.191
n Dom	1125	2.111
n Aff	1750.5	3.284

Summary Statistics	
DF	3
# Samples	4
# Cases	533
Chi-Sq	278.04
Chi-Sq (corrected for ties)	298.557
$p < .001$	

Source: Ross, 1991

therefore be reasonably concluded that members of this particular group are the ones more likely to attain employment in this industry. They are highly motivated to do so, exhibit confidence in their own ability to achieve their goals and are prepared to work in order to attain their desired ends. Such characteristics all point towards higher levels of job attainment, particularly positions associated with higher levels of salary, work satisfaction and career progression.

Higher levels of the need for Autonomy and the need for Dominance were found to be associated with a confidence in attaining desired tourism/hospitality employment and willingness to engage in further study on leaving school. Thus higher levels of this form of vocational self-confidence and preparedness for further study would seem to be associated with the three personality needs of Achievement, Autonomy and Dominance. The personality need of Affiliation did not emerge as being associated with these measures of employment in the tourism/hospitality industry. It may be that while Affiliation is an important need in the actual workplace, in the motivation of potential employees to seek employment in this industry it does not play a major instrumental role.

A willingness to seek post-secondary school training was found to be clearly associated with higher levels of the need for Achievement. Moreover, such individuals recognised the value of obtaining training experiences in various parts of the world, and were not satisfied with perhaps a parochial understanding of training. Such individuals may not only be indicating an international understanding of employment prospects in regard to this industry, but may also demonstrate a greater liking for and perhaps a greater resilience in the face of the often transient and peripatetic employment nature of the tourism/hospitality industry. Thus such individuals may be more likely to survive and thrive in this industry.

Finally, this study has revealed that females have demonstrated higher levels of motivation to attain tourism/hospitality employment and higher levels of tourism/hospitality industry job success estimation at all levels of the need for Achievement. It may thus be concluded that females with a higher need for Achievement are more likely to be attracted to and seek employment in this industry and be more confident of employment attainment. Such a finding may in part suggest that employment in the tourism/hospitality industry is still seen by many males as not as desirable as law, medicine, or engineering. It may be that female students are not as encumbered by such traditional vocational stereotypes, and are more likely to see this major and growing industry as a potential career source. Such vocational stereotypes may serve only to disadvantage males in the swiftly changing employment market of many countries in the light of the rapidly expanding leisure and tourism/hospitality industries.

This study has found evidence to suggest that personality variables do play a predictive role in the understanding of vocational intention in regard to the tourism/hospitality industry. It may be that there are other personality variables that also play a predictive role here. Introversion/extroversion may be one such domain. There would also now seem to be a need to explore these results in other tourism/hospitality contexts around the world, examining issues such as a possible age-level dependency of these findings and their applicability to the various work contexts that make up the tourism/hospitality employment scene. It would also seem that the tourism/hospitality industry may need to pay greater attention to its potential workforce, supplying more, and more accurate information about its work environment to schools and colleges if it is to attract those individuals whose personality disposition maximally equips them for career options in this industry.

Anglo-Greek tourism career perceptions

Career perceptions in regard to tourism employment has recently been examined by Airey and Frontistis (1997) among both United Kingdom and Greek school students. These researchers have examined the context within which tourism career perceptions are formed and decisions are made. They have scrutinised both perceptions of tourism and also specific attitudes towards tourism jobs, and have found that United Kingdom respondents have both a better established careers support system (i.e. guidance counsellors) and also a less positive attitude towards tourism than had Greek respondents. The authors conclude that the United Kingdom respondents had a somewhat more realistic view of the nature of tourism jobs generally. Airey and Frontistis conclude that careers support and education for tourism is considerably more developed in the United Kingdom than in Greece, and that the United Kingdom system generally works efficiently in the provision of both broad and realistic views of career options to young people. In contrast, they suggest that Greece does not, at this point, possess the same degree of support able to be directed towards potential tourism workers. They conclude that one result of this deficiency was that Greek young people appeared to them to be at a less informed, perhaps a 'fantasy' stage in their conceptualisation of careers. The authors go on to suggest that Greek young people are more likely to exhibit a glamorous and unrealistic view of tourism careers than their United Kingdom counterparts, because of this fantasy stage of career conceptualisation. Young people in the United Kingdom, they found, are generally more hostile or negative in their attitudes towards tourism career paths. They conclude that other factors may help to account for these attitudinal divergences. Differences in relative levels of experience as tourists may also account for some of the contrast, as many differences in the employment structures of the two countries.

Airey and Frontistis have also documented important differences between views about employment in tourism as a whole, as well as views about individual tourism jobs. They have found that when surveyed in regard to specific jobs, the attitudes of United Kingdom young people emerged as more positive than many of their Greek counterparts. They conclude that it is more realistic to elicit responses to individual jobs, and that such responses are likely to be more accurate and informative than more general responses relating to tourism as a whole. These researchers have also reported findings related to the different perceptions regarding that which is perceived to constitute the tourism sector. They report that there were notable omissions and contrasts in young peoples' perceptions as to that which constitutes a tourism job. They point to the low level of identification in both the United Kingdom and also Greece of many positions in the accommodation and catering sector as being part of the tourism industry. They found such findings both surprising and also indicative of a deficiency in the provision of careers information about the tourism industry. They conclude that an important task lies ahead for many people in the tourism industry to attend to semantic issues.

Summary

This chapter has explored major theoretical conceptualisations of work behaviour from the domain of psychology. The chapter has examined the value of fundamental concepts from human resource management/organisational psychology which could be applied to tourism/hospitality industry employment. Findings from recent studies have then amplified some of these notions as they illuminate behaviour and motivation within the tourism/hospitality industry employment context.

CHAPTER 7 DISCUSSION TOPICS

Describe Maslow's motivational hierarchy as applied to the work place.

Outline the four major work motivators within McClelland's schema.

Discuss the role of values in work motivation.

Examine the role of satisfaction in the Valued Job Attributes/Actual Job Attributes fit.

Describe major personality needs associated with a preference for tourism/hospitality industry employment.

How do perceptions of the tourism industry differ among young people in the United Kingdom and in Greece?

8

Evaluation of Tourism Facilities

LEARNING OBJECTIVES

An understanding of:

- Methodological and conceptual issues associated with evaluation research.
- Major research issues within the domain of environmental evaluation.
- Applications of evaluation research to the tourism context.
- Communication processes in environmental interpretation and museum visitation.

V isitor evaluation within tourist/leisure contexts, particularly museums, has long been a research interest within psychology. A number of environmental psychology texts apportion considerable space to this topic (see Proshanky, Ittelson and Rivlin 1976; Fisher, Bell and Baum 1984; Bell, Fisher and Loomis 1989). A good deal of the research is best described as visitor reactions to environmental design, and the reactions studied range from the specific aspects of the design (O'Hare 1974; Lakota 1975), to museum fatigue (Melton 1972) to exit bias (Bell, Fisher and Loomis 1978), through to overall reactions to the visitor centre (Countryside Commission 1979; Washbourne and Wagar 1972). This chapter will cover various theoretical topics from the domain of social and environmental psychology as they are of relevance to the evaluation of the tourist context. The chapter will then highlight studies which have investigated major theoretical concepts applied to visitor behaviour.

Evaluation research

Babbie (1992) has pointed out that evaluation research — sometimes called program evaluation — refers to a research purpose rather than a specific research method. Its special purpose is to evaluate the impact of social interventions in a wide variety of settings. Many methods — surveys, experiments, and so on — can be used in evaluation research. Evaluation research is probably as old as social science research generally. Whenever people have instituted a social reform for a specific purpose, they have paid attention to its actual consequences, even if they have not always done so in a conscious, deliberate, or sophisticated fashion. In recent years, however, the field of evaluation research has become an increasingly popular and active research specialty, which has been reflected in textbooks, courses, and projects. The growth of evaluation research, for Babbie, also indicates a more general trend in the social sciences. As a consequence, it is said, one is likely to read increasing numbers of evaluation reports, and tourism researchers are likely to be asked to conduct such evaluations.

In part, the growth of evaluation research no doubt reflects tourism researchers' increasing desire to actually make a valued impact in the tourism industry. At the same time, one cannot discount the influence of (1) increased government requirements for program evaluations to accompany the implementation of new programs and (2) the availability of government research funds to fulfil that requirement. Whatever the mixture of these influences, it seems clear that tourism researchers will be bringing their evaluation skills into the tourism world more in the future than ever before. Babbie (1992) makes the point that in evaluation research, formulating questions is as important as answering them. Evaluation research, since it occurs within real life, is said to have special problems. There are particular logistical problems as well as special ethical issues involved in evaluation research generally, and in its specific technical procedures. As any researcher reports on program evaluations, he/she should be especially sensitive to these logistical problems. Evaluation is also said to be a form of applied research — it is intended to have some real-world effect. It is useful, therefore, to consider whether and how it is actually applied. The clear and obvious implications of an evaluation research project do not necessarily have any impact on real life. They may become the focus of ideological, rather than scientific, debates. According to Babbie they may simply be denied out of hand, as occurs when individuals or organisations summarily dismiss the conclusions drawn by evaluation studies.

Conceptual issues in evaluation

As a first step in the understanding of the process of evaluation it is said by Babbie to be necessary to organise the concept of evaluation into meaningful categories which can be used for the intelligent planning of appropriate evaluation activities. Although outcome evaluation has often been differentiated from other types of evaluation, Babbie believes that the structure of outcome evaluation itself has not been adequately explored. Efforts have been made to develop, categorise and assess research designs which can be of use to evaluators (Cook and Campbell 1976; Hatry, Winnie and Fisk 1973; Isaac and Michael 1974). The concept of outcome evaluation, however, has been regarded as transcending the boundaries of research design. Consequently, any attempt to understand the value of outcome evaluation solely in terms of a methodological critique is said to be bound to yield incomplete and often misleading information. Thus a major task of this section will be to present a multi-dimensional typology of outcome evaluation which can serve as a comprehensive approach to planning evaluation studies which may be used in tourism/hospitality settings.

Evaluation typology can be organised around three basic questions, according to Babbie. First, what are the types of evaluation that are carried out at present, and what are the relative merits of each type? Second, how can the validity of each type be optimised? Third, how can the usefulness of each type be optimised? Three categories of evaluation type and four categories of evaluation usefulness can be conceptualised. Evaluation type can be seen in terms of 'client-type comparison' studies, 'follow-up' studies and 'modality tests'. Evaluation usefulness, it is said, can be dealt with in terms of an evaluation plan's ability to help establish realistic expectations, to improve service over the short term, to help with long-range planning, and to be of value in the political arena. Although the concepts of type, validity and usefulness are related, there is a large amount of independence among them. For Babbie each type of evaluation may be carried out in a more or less valid manner. Although one type of evaluation may be better than another on some scale of validity, it is also true that within the limitations of each method, validity can vary a great deal. This perspective is said to be particularly important because the demands of particular situations may suggest the use of one or another type of evaluation. By considering evaluation type and evaluation validity separately, one is not forced into insisting on an inappropriate evaluation plan merely to satisfy the demands of adequate validity. 'Type of evaluation' and 'validity of evaluation' are said to be reasonably independent of each other. They are said to be, at least, independent enough that it makes sense to deal with each as a separate consideration in any attempt to assess the value of an evaluation plan.

The validity and the usefulness of an evaluation must also, according to Babbie, be considered as separate entities. The literature on research utilisation makes it quite clear that a host of factors other than validity or scientific value are involved in the determination of which evaluation studies will be important. A few of the more important factors are the relevance of the information, the source of the information, compatibility between suggested change and organisational structure, difficulty of implementation, and the makeup of an organisation's staff. It is said that it is sometimes difficult to find mention of issues concerning scientific validity in discussions of crucial factors in the utilisation of research or evaluation data. If an evaluation is to have maximum impact, factors related to utilisation must be considered in the design stage, and these factors must be dealt with in their own right rather than as adjuncts to the matter of research validity (Babbie, 1992).

A common problem with the development and implementation of evaluation for Babbie is a feeling on the part of service delivery, management or planning personnel that the evaluation in which they must participate is irrelevant. Such opinions may well be correct. They are said to arise when evaluators draw up plans which fail to consider adequately issues of usefulness. One reason for such failure might be an undue concern with validity or type of evaluation, and an attendant failure to realise that evaluation usefulness does not automatically derive from an appropriate or valid evaluation study. Usefulness is a complex issue which should be dealt with in its own right. An important consequence of considering one element to the exclusion of others is a frustrating and futile attempt to force a square peg into a round hole — an inappropriate evaluation design into a particular evaluation setting.

The technological nature of program evaluation

Superimposed upon the three-dimensional structure of outcome evaluation is said by Babbie to be the matter of the technological as opposed to the scientific nature of evaluation research. Much time and effort is said to be wasted as a result of attempts to use evaluation to add to the body of social science knowledge, or to transpose directly scientific methods and theories into the technological endeavour that is evaluation. This problem is said to be particularly serious because the scientific enterprise is not optimally suited to the task of effecting the types of changes that are desired by those who might fund tourism/hospitality research. Scientific models are said not likely to produce information that is directly applicable to the improvement of industry programs. Babbie believes that the relationship between social science and the technology of improving industry programs is at best convoluted, diffuse, and indirect. Although there are important and beneficial interactions between these areas of endeavour, those benefits cannot be fully appreciated until the relationship between science and technology is understood and the limits of each are defined. The most useful designs in the three-dimensional 'evaluation space' are those which are technological rather than scientific in character, but which fully exploit relevant elements of social science. Thus, for Babbie, a thorough understanding of the technological model of evaluation complements the 'type' validity-usefulness model, and together they provide a highly effective guide to the choice of optimally valuable evaluation plans.

Evaluation implementation issues

While 'evaluation space' and technological models may be sufficient according to Babbie for the design of powerful evaluation studies, they are said to be inadequate as guides to the implementation of those studies. Since evaluation must actually be implemented before it can help solve social problems, a further step in developing a powerful evaluation is an analysis of the implementation problem. It is extremely difficult to carry out evaluation in ongoing social programs, and many evaluators find themselves trapped by forces which they do not understand and cannot control. Babbie believes that since the quality of an evaluation plan is no guarantee of its use, it is important to focus specific attention on the problems of implementation. Those problems are part of a general historical and sociological context which affects the relationship between social science and industry, and an analysis may profitably proceed within that general framework. It should demonstrate why problems exist, why those problems are difficult to solve, and how solutions might be affected. Babbie argues that developing powerful new evaluation paradigms will almost certainly have consequences for the professional structure of social research. Some of those consequences are said to be likely to be counterproductive both for evaluation and for society at large, and one must be ready to counteract difficulties which may arise. A tourism/hospitality industry evaluator therefore must anticipate such problems, understand why they are likely to occur, and explore what can be done about them.

Museum research

Research on the educational effectiveness and enjoyment of museums and exhibitions has been a prominent feature of work within the fields of communication and design for a number of decades now. Within the discipline of psychology, notions such as right-handed bias, exit phenomenon/exit gradient, and information overload/museum fatigue have long been the subject of investigation and comment. The right-handed bias effect refers to the tendency of visitors to museums to turn right upon entering a gallery or exhibit hall and move around in that direction (Robinson 1928; Melton 1972). The exit phenomenon or exit gradient refers to the tendency of visitors to use the first exit they encounter in a museum and in so doing often miss parts of the museum (Parsons and Loomis 1973). Museums have been found to produce information overload and hence museum fatigue, if for example, the exhibits are too complex or it is difficult to move around easily among the various displays (Melton 1972). Melton also found that once inside a museum people stop at the first few exhibits and then become more selective, stopping at fewer the longer they explore. Melton also made the point that those items or displays which are then observed tend to hold greater interest for the visitor. The degree of interest here Melton termed attraction gradient.

Environmental evaluation

Mehrabian (1972) and Mehrabian and Russell (1974) have persuasively argued that individuals evaluate the environment surrounding them according to a number of basic factors. These factors represent fundamental emotional experiences or dimensions of emotional operation. Mehrabian and Russell would hold that each of these dimensions is bipolar in nature, having opposite meanings. For the first evaluative dimension, which they label Pleasure, the positive end of the continuum may be represented by words such as happy, pleased, contented, satisfied and hopeful. The negative end of this dimension may be represented by words such as unhappy, annoyed, and unsatisfied. Within the context of tourist evaluation, activities which are believed to fall at the negative end of the Pleasure dimension may well be avoided by tourists or would engender complaints if they were compelled to engage in them. The second dimension is one of Arousal. Again, this has two ends or poles: the positive end being a point where the person feels stimulated, wide-awake, aroused, excited and even frenzied. The negative end of this dimension, where the expression negative is used to imply opposite rather than undesirable, is characterised by emotional states where one is relaxed, calm, sluggish, sleepy, bored and even dull. Mehrabian and Russell hold that there is a third important dimension, that of Dominance, which is also needed to describe any emotional reaction to an environment. Terms to describe the positive end of the dominance dimension include controlling, influential, important, in control, dominant; while the opposite end of this dimension involves feelings of being controlled, being cared for, being guided, feeling submissive and being awed. Finally, Mehrabian and Russell argue that these dimensions or emotional domains are independent of each other in that an individual may evaluate an activity as being high on one dimension, e.g. pleasure, but low on another, e.g. dominance.

Relatively little has thus far been achieved regarding a thorough application of this evaluative schema to tourist behaviour. One study, however, has achieved some success in this area. Pearce (1985), in a study of visitor activity ratings on a Great Barrier Reef island, found that this three-factor evaluative schema produced a diverse spread of activity ratings within the three-dimensional space. He reports that while there were variations in the extent of pleasure obtained from each activity, generally the activities were seen as pleasurable. However, for the other two dimensions there was a greater diversity in classification. Some activities were seen as exciting, while others were not so exciting; some of these same activities dominant, others not dominant. Pearce makes the point that while there are some individual differences in emotional reaction for each visitor to the various activities, the value of this schema lies in its ability to provide an estimate of the general profile for each tourist activity along these evaluative dimensions. Among the more important concepts within the domain of environmental evaluation are authenticity and person-environment fit. The following sections will provide a coverage of these two important areas.

Authenticity

It has been argued by commentators such as MacCannell (1973) and Pearce (1982, 1985) that the notion of authenticity provides us with one of the most important insights into the behaviour of tourists. Tysoe (1985) has written of the widespread belief that tourists are basically shallow and foolish individuals, typically satisfied with superficial, staged, unauthentic glimpses into the life of the country or region they are visiting. In similar vein, commentators such as Boorstin (1964) and later Turner and Ash (1975) see tourism as essentially an aberration, a symptom of the malaise of the times. They bemoan the disappearance of the traveller of old, who they believe was in search of authentic experiences, and deprecate the modern tourist who they see as searching for and experiencing only pseudo or staged events.

In contrast with these views are those of MacCannell (1973, 1976) who would see many tourists and travellers as seeking authentic and genuine contact with the people and places they visit, and that few visitors seek superficial or contrived experiences. Pearce and Moscardo (1985) have found evidence to suggest a link between authenticity on the one hand and levels of travel career. Here higher levels of authenticity were related to wishes to achieve higher levels of personal motivation as reflected in concepts such as self-actualisation, whereas lower levels of interest in authenticity or genuineness were related to interest in primarily satisfying biologically related drives such as hunger or thirst or needs such as shelter. Pearce and Moscardo have further found that those tourists who were more likely to express motivation concerned with self-esteem or self-actualisation were less likely to be satisfied with staged or unauthentic experiences than were those tourists more concerned to satisfy biological or shelter concerns. Thus the notion of authenticity has been found to be of some use in the understanding of aspects of tourist behaviour. Pearce and Moscardo (1986) in a further exploration of authenticity as a useful explanatory notion within tourism studies, have argued for research involving authenticity and concepts such as social status, self-worth, and interpersonal relationships among tourists and locals.

Person-environment fit

Pearce and Moscardo (1984) have written that the notion of person-environment fit is an important one in the understanding of tourist behaviour. The person-environment fit concept has received extensive treatment in the writings of Argyle, Furnham and Graham (1981), and Furnham and Argyle (1981).

There has been ample evidence gathered to suggest that individuals deliberately seek situations which they feel match their personalities and interests. Pearce and Moscardo believe that this finding is particularly apposite to tourist settings wherein individuals make a conscious choice regarding a holiday in a particular setting or destination. They also believe that, on occasions, individuals may find themselves in contexts which do not match their personalities, values or interests. Such a situation is likely to evoke discomfort and complaint. The task in such a situation is to diminish the possibility of a mismatch between the goals of visitors and the leisure environment chosen. Pearce and Moscardo argue that an investigation of the advertising and marketing practices of the leisure environment may be the more appropriate procedure here in many instances.

Methodological issues

This section will examine measurement issues and procedures associated with topics such as visitor satisfaction and learning within the domain of visitor evaluation in an historical leisure context.

Measurement of visitor reactions

Perhaps the most popular form of instrument in the assessment of tourist feedback is the visitor questionnaire, usually a pencil-and-paper measure completed by guests around the time of departure. Lewis and Pizam (1981) have written that this technique provides a quick measure of overall guest satisfaction, that it can identify dimensions in which satisfaction or dissatisfaction occurs, and that it can identify individual determinants that comprise each dimension and which might be the specific causes of satisfaction or dissatisfaction. They argue that the questionnaire is easily completed by most guests, and may be speedily tabulated and analysed by management. Lewis and Pizam further argue that the result may be a valid and reliable method for rating management, locating operational malfunctions, ascertaining guests' needs and comparisons among leisure installations, and gauging improvements or deteriorations over time. Finally, Lewis and Pizam hold that the survey instrument should be used with some caution, operationalising more sophisticated concepts in questions, and generally employing the more powerful analysis techniques such as multivariate analyses. Pearce and Moscardo (1984) make the point that the study of tourist complaints and negative experiences is also an appropriate method within the context of tourist evaluation. They have written that tourists' complaints are most often collected by way of techniques such as visitors' books, guest cards and questionnaires, along with interpersonal contact with staff.

Evaluation of interpretation centres

Pearce and Moscardo (1985) make the point that within visitor evaluation two components may be distinguished: visitor profiles and visitor reactions. Visitor profiles have traditionally been the favoured aim for many proprietors or guardians of a recreational area who want to know more about the people who use their facility. However, visitor reactions are increasingly seen as important, for they reflect tourists' cognitions, their satisfactions and emotional reactions to the specific tourist venue, and it is this type of evaluation upon which this section will focus. Pearce and Moscardo have examined the research evidence associated with visitor centres in various contexts and locations. They report that visitor centres are usually constructed adjacent to the venue of interest, and often are a prelude to visiting the park or environment itself. They hold that exhibits in a visitor centre are meant to interpret, to comment upon and stimulate interest and enjoyment in the environment the tourist is about to visit. They argue that the chief aim of the visitor centre is interpretation, which may be defined as the stimulation of tourist interest and enthusiasm, and the educational or pedagogic supplement to satisfy that interest.

The study of interpretation centres, particularly in contexts such as national parks, has been of some interest to researchers over the last two decades (e.g. Washbourne and Wagar 1972). However, it is the research of the Countryside Commission (1979) in the United Kingdom that is particularly apposite in the present context. This work utilised a psychological framework in its assessment of visitor centres, and recognised that the central product offered by any tourist location is 'experience', a point recently emphasised by commentators such as Iso-Ahola (1980). The Countryside Commission looked at visitor understanding, enjoyment, and motivation, and attempted to relate these factors by way of the examination of display variables and visitor demographics. One of the findings of this study was that enjoyment and understanding are apparently relatively unrelated: people may enjoy their visit to a tourist site without necessarily learning a great deal from it. The study also found that the greatest amount of learning occurred at historical centres, whereas high levels of enjoyment were reported by the visitors at all centres. The highest enjoyment was reported at those locations where visitors could inspect the site as well as learn about it in the interpretation centre.

The study further found that factors such as size and layout of the centre, or the provision of an audio-visual program on the theme of the centre did not seem to relate to visitor enjoyment. The centres that motivated visitors to learn more about the park or venue were usually large and used a number of different types of interpretation. They also report that animated, physically involving dynamic displays were found to be most effective in capturing the attention of all ages and social backgrounds. One finding which did emerge from this study, and which has been considered by Pearce and Moscardo (1985), and Moscardo (1991) is that which concerns enjoyment without accompanying learning. The results of studies such as that by the Countryside Commission have revealed that sometimes little information is taken in by many visitors, yet most report that they are quite satisfied by their experiences at the site. Pearce and Moscardo suggest, as a possible explanation, the operation of a general psychological construct termed 'mindlessness'. Drawing upon the work of Langer (Chanowitz and Langer 1980), they argue that much apparently thoughtful action is mindless, where the term is defined as a mental state in which there is little questioning of new information, and where individuals are mentally passive and are processing their surroundings by way of pre-existing scripts and routines. Mindfulness, on the other hand, is said to be characterised by a more analytic and detailed attention to task or surroundings. Moreover, mindfulness is said to be associated with more efficient recall of experience and acquired information. The relevance of this psychological theory to tourist evaluation, Pearce and Moscardo argue, may be in the hypothesis that some tourists may be processing the exhibits, and indeed the park itself, mindlessly. They go on to argue that visitors would be even more satisfied with their experiences if they interacted with their environment mindfully. In support of this, they cite the finding that many visitors preferred exhibits with greater activity and involvement, and reported highest satisfaction levels in such situations.

Moscardo and Pearce (1986) have since reanalysed the Countryside Commission's (1979) data, so as to explore direct and indirect relationships among variables such as enjoyment, learning and mindfulness. Their analyses have revealed a number of interesting and notable associations. The Countryside Commission had concluded that there was little or no association between enjoyment and information gain. However, Moscardo and Pearce found that when variables such as age, education and size of group were controlled for in the analysis, the correlation increased considerably. They also found a direct correlation between enjoyment and mindfulness, and concluded that centres with historical themes were the ones most likely to demonstrate high positive associations among variables such as enjoyment, information recall, mindfulness, and subjective judgements of knowledge gained.

The next section explores related conceptualisations within a museum visitor context, and extends the examination of notions such as mindfulness, informativeness, perceptions of subjective learning and knowledge alongside evaluative dimensions such as levels of excitement, enjoyment and authenticity.

Museum scripts

Moscardo (1991) has pointed out that museums are major tourist attractions, and tourists are increasingly seeking educational value from them. This is putting pressure on museums to provide a range of effective educational experiences. She points out that there is already a long tradition of psychological research in museums. Her work has been concerned both with the use of museums as non-laboratory settings to investigate cognitive concepts and theories, and also to provide information for the better design of exhibits and museums. As such, her studies represent an innovative application of current theoretical concepts to the overall evaluation of museum contexts. A model to describe the museum visit and predict visitor behaviour and cognition has been generated by Moscardo. This model is based on Langer's mindfulness/mindlessness concept. The model basically predicts that the individual script for a museum visit is likely not to include elements concerned with learning or processing information, labelled as MBUILD or MTRANS elements (from Schank and Abelson 1977). Moscardo's study has examined the descriptions of a museum visit by 348 subjects so as to document and analyse museum script content within a number of Australian museums. Her results have suggested that the museum script includes relatively few MBUILD or MTRANS elements, and finds strong support for the mindfulness/mindlessness model when applied to museum visitation. Moscardo's study has also provided evidence to suggest that scripts differ according to experience: whether respondents have direct or vicarious experience of the situation.

Moscardo basically found that the concept of mindlessness fits Australian museum visitor behaviour data well. Her observational studies suggest that visitors develop a script for behaving in a museum which involves walking to exhibits, looking briefly at exhibits, and then moving to the next exhibit. Other predictions from the mindlessness/mindfulness approach to cognitive activity are also found to be supported by museum research results. This approach predicts that people will become mindful whenever they encounter unexpected, unfamiliar, or surprising elements in a setting, when they are given the opportunity to participate in an activity, or when the information in an environment is very important or relevant to them (Moscardo 1991).

Moscardo concludes that understanding the content and structure of a museum visit script can provide a variety of answers to complex theoretical questions regarding visitor behaviour. She points out that several authors (Ross 1987; Cohen 1979, Pearce 1988) have argued that research into visitor or tourist behaviour should be emic, contextual, processual and longitudinal. In particular, Ross (1987) and Pearce (1988) have emphasised the need to examine tourists' understanding and expectations of their behaviour and of the setting under study. She points out that Pearce (1984) has highlighted the value of examining in detail the concepts and cognitive structures of tourists for understanding difficulties which can arise in social situations encountered by tourists. Overall, the results of Moscardo's study indicated that the script for a museum visit was a very basic set of three elements — arrive at the museum, look at the exhibits, and leave. These were the only three actions included in descriptions of a visit to a museum by more than one-third of the sample. She concludes that it is likely in a more structured approach more elements would be regarded as important for a visit to a museum, but the three listed above would appear to be the only actions in a museum visit that are sufficiently salient to be included in an unstructured description. She further points out that this script fits the patterns obtained in actual observations of visitors.

Moscardo has further found that the study revealed differences between the scripts of various groups. The scripts of those who have never been to a museum suggest that museum visitors do not expect to think or learn in their visit, and this may partly explain why they then do not appear to pay much attention to the information provided in museums. While experience with museum visits was found to be linked to higher rates of inclusion for various actions that could be MBUILD or MTRANS elements, the action of think or learn was still not seen by more than 80% of the sample as sufficiently important or critical to the experience to be included in description of a museum visit (Moscardo 1991).

Moscardo has pointed out that some results of interest to individuals such as museum professionals and educators are likely to be the differences found between adults and children, and between males and females. All children sampled believed that a museum visit involved seeing dinosaurs and/or old bones. This reflected both their experiences with museums and the image museums have in the media and literature. She highlights the potential for disappointment among children in not finding these objects in a museum. She also notes that very few children (6.3%) saw museums as places for thinking or learning, yet children had a much higher inclusion rate (23.8%) for interacting with exhibits. Many children's museums and galleries use exhibits designed to be interactive, and these exhibits are often claimed to require mental as well as motor activity on the part of the child. She notes that the inclusion rate for thinking and learning elements might have been higher for children.

In regard to differences based on sex, the results indicated that females were consistently more likely to include MBUILD or MTRANS elements. Elsewhere (Argyle et al. 1981) she points out that females have been found to be more sensitive to subtle social cues and that this may have been more influenced by a social desirability bias to include these elements. She provides an

Table 8.1 Frequency distribution for inclusion of actions in descriptions for four motives for visit groups

Action	Relaxation	Entertain-ment	Education	Family Outing
	%	%	%	%
Arrive	36.6	40.4	37.5	45.5
Pay	22.0	14.0	20.5	11.4
Get pamphlets	26.8	26.3	33.0	27.3
Look at a map	22.0	22.8	19.6	20.5
Take a guided tour	4.9	5.3	5.4	6.8
Decide on a plan for visit	14.6	24.6	20.5	18.2
Get to exhibits	29.3	40.4	35.7	22.7
Read labels	17.1	22.8	17.9	15.9
Think/learn	12.2	10.5	23.2	9.1*
Look at exhibits	82.9	77.2	77.7	79.5
Watch film/ audiovisual	2.4	7.0	4.5	4.5
Interact with exhibits	–	5.3	3.6	2.3
Discuss visit/exhibits with companions	12.2	17.5	20.5	40.9*
Rest	2.4	3.5	5.4	6.8
Ask staff questions	9.8	3.5	13.4	6.8
Go to bookshop	2.4	7.0	17.9	6.8*
Go to coffee shop/ restaurant	12.2	19.3	17.0	22.7
Leave	34.1	40.4	47.3	38.6
	(n = 41)	(n = 57)	(n = 11)	(n = 44)

* Chi-square significant, p < .01

Source: Moscardo (1991)

alternative explanation which is that females may visit museums with different groups. Perhaps they are more likely to visit with children and are thus more concerned with the educational aspects of museums. Moscardo concludes that this is partly supported both by the finding that females were more likely to visit with family and friends, and that those who go to a museum for the purpose of a family outing are more likely to include the element of discussion of the museum/exhibits with companions.

Moscardo has also explored the notion of motivation in this context. One group of questions guiding the study was concerned with the possible inclusion of MBUILD or MTRANS elements in the museum visit script. She found that some respondents did include in their museum visit descriptions, actions which could have been seen as MBUILD or MTRANS elements, but the highest percentage of inclusion for the total sample was 23.9% for the action of getting pamphlets. Moscardo found that only 13.8% included any action involving thinking or learning about the material in the museum. Even when respondents explicitly stated that they had an educational purpose for their museum visit, she found only 23.3% included the think or learn action. Table 8.1 contains a cross-tabulation of motivation by type of action.

She concludes that the examination of the content of a museum visit script supports the proposal that museum visitors are often mindless, and this is consistent with the results of previous survey and observational research (see Moscardo 1988). This study also provides support for the mindlessness/mindfulness model for visitor behaviour and cognition. In summary, Moscardo's study has used the concept of scripts to guide an investigation of what people see as necessary to describe a museum visit. This study is in the tradition of previous theoretical and evaluative research in museums and in other areas of psychology and tourism (see Pearce 1988), and has obtained results of considerable applied and theoretical value. Her results also were directed at several substantive areas to be addressed by museum educators, such as the images of museums in media and literature and the issue of orientation systems for museums. Moscardo's results have also provided support for further research into ways to improve museum exhibits and design, so as to increase visitors' cognitive activity and enjoyment in what are now regarded as very important resources for the tourism industry.

Visitor enjoyment and museum visitation

Schouten (1995) has pointed out that in the last few decades there has been an enormous increase in the attendance figures of museums. A closer look at the statistics, however, is said to show that the number of visits has been growing, rather than the number of visitors. Frequent users, Schouten argues, are using museums even more frequently, but new audiences are hardly reached. Museums are still regarded as not for them.

Schouten suggests a variety of cogent reasons for this misconception:

- The world represented by museums is not the world as perceived by the general public. It is a world structured by scientific laws, by taxonomy and by a division in periods which is not at all common ground for the lay-person. Museum professionals tend to forget that what is obvious to them is not clear to anyone else.

- In a museum all the objects tend to look alike to the non-specialist, especially if they are piled up in large quantities.
- The communication in museums is rather conventional: everyone is presumed to start from the same point and to undergo the same knowledge-enhancing experience at the same pace. Thus the visitor plays the passive role and the museum the active role. Access to museums is highly structured, predetermined and controlled by the staff so as to be 'correct', 'understandable' and 'educational'.
- There is a myth that visitors come to learn something in a museum. However, every visitor does not come to museums, visitor centres and heritage sites to learn something, although they still insist on saying so in all the visitor surveys. Their behaviour in the galleries is more akin to window-shopping on a Saturday afternoon than to the intelligent acquisition of new knowledge. The public are kind enough not to complain, partly because it is very difficult for them to formulate any alternative as they are not experts in the field of the objects displayed, and partly because — and this is a more serious problem — they believe scientific knowledge needs to be presented in a remote and abstract way.
- Related to the above myth is the neglected fact that one of the most important reasons to visit museums is the opportunity for social interaction. A visit to an exhibition is a social occasion. Visitors hardly ever come alone, they present themselves in small groups as a family, a group of friends, etc. Visiting the displays is said to be a means to interact with each other. Shouten here makes an extremely important point.

Shouten summarises by arguing that learning is done by people who are curious, who wonder about the world around them, and not by people who might be intimidated by so-called educational displays. A lot of the communication in interpretation centres and museums is said not to be inviting but just pedantic. In most cases the assessment of the heritage attraction is not based on the scientific correctness of the core product, but on how effective the site or the exhibition is in raising curiosity, appealing to fantasy and in providing a challenge, as well as on items such as: how clean the toilets are, how easy it is to park the car, the choice of items in the shop and the quality of the catering. Shouten cogently argues that these are also among the critical quality features the management should turn into success features.

Summary

This chapter has provided an examination of the major theoretical concepts from disciplines such as psychology as they may be applied to the evaluation of tourist contexts and sites. It has been demonstrated that notions such as authenticity, person-environment fit and mindfulness-mindlessness are of major utility in the understanding of visitor preferences and behaviours. The chapter has also explored some of these issues within recent museum evaluation research, providing a reference point and springboard for the application of these important theoretical conceptualisations within other tourist contexts.

CHAPTER 8 DISCUSSION TOPICS

Describe the major typologies of evaluation research.

Outline Mehrabian's dimensions of environmental evaluation.

Assess the role of authenticity as highlighted by tourism evaluation research.

Explore the roles of learning and enjoyment in visitor experiences.

How have notions such as mindfulness/mindlessness been investigated among museum visitors?

Assess the importance of social interaction in successful museum management.

9

The Social
Impacts of
Tourism

LEARNING OBJECTIVES

An understanding of:

- The fundamental processes concerned with stability and change at work in any community.
- The types and variety of impact studies in the tourism arena.
- Models of impact outcomes.
- Research strategies employed in a variety of contexts.
- Community-focused research on the social impacts of tourism.
- The role of friendliness perceptions in host-visitor relationships.

This chapter will focus on one of the more sensitive issues emerging in applied tourism research, that of social impacts of tourism on host communities. The chapter will provide an introduction to social changes in communities due to tourism growth, some of the mechanisms associated with community functioning, impacts of tourism as well as stress models. The chapter then concludes with the presentation of studies of tourism's social impacts on host cities.

The context of social impacts

Over the last few years a number of communities have experienced a quite considerable growth in tourist numbers. Indeed the popularity of countries such as Australia as a tourist destination has increased rapidly, with overseas arrivals doubling between 1986 and 1988. By the year 2001 it is expected to double in size again, and reach over 5 million (Bureau of Tourism Research 1993). Such changes in the economic and social life of many communities cannot but have an impact upon residents whether for good or ill. Mathieson and Wall (1982) have written that large-scale developments as a consequence of tourist growth are likely to have profound effects upon the lives of many members of host communities. Murphy (1985) has argued that two contrasting situations can evolve from tourist development, representing co-ordinates along a social interaction continuum. At one extreme, tourism-related social changes can lead to development, representing socio-economic advances in the community, an improvement in the standard of living, and an overall social and cultural enrichment in the life of a city which leads to perceptions of social and economic well-being. At the other extreme, changes can lead to dependency, represented by economic growth which leaves an underdeveloped social structure or reinforces and enhances existing social injustices. In this latter situation, Murphy holds that a few members of the host community gain handsomely from the growth and development, whereas the majority of the residents do not participate in or benefit economically or socially in any meaningful way from the industry. Such a situation can lead to feelings of resentment, bitterness and expressions of hostility towards fellow residents and visitors.

While most governments around the world focus principally upon positive economic benefits, there is now increasing recognition of the potential social and environmental costs associated with tourist development (Lui, Sheldon and Var 1987), and the necessity for a careful investigation of non-economic effects (Allen, Long, Perdue and Kieselbach 1988; Lui, Sheldon and Var 1987; Murphy 1981). Cooke (1982) and Loukissas (1983) have called for careful tourism planning aimed at minimising tourism's negative impacts and maximising benefits for host community members. They, together with many other commentators, point out that for a tourism industry to survive, residents must be favourably disposed to tourists. Cooke, for example, argues that residents must be involved, and perceive that they exercise some influence within the planning process. In a similar vein, Allen *et al.* (1988) have also advocated that residents' attitudes towards tourist impacts on community life should be constantly monitored, and problems promptly rectified in favour of the host community.

Models of community functioning

Heller, Price, Reinharz, Rigor, Wandersman and D'Aunno (1984) have made the point that community psychology has produced a great diversity of models by which community structures and functioning may be explored and understood. During the 1960s and 1970s perhaps the most prominent model related to mental health, as expounded by Cooke (1970), Mann (1978) and Morrison (1979). However, this is by no means the only context or set of formulations by which community processes have been comprehended. Heller *et al.* (1984) and Mann (1978) have written of ecological and social action models within community psychology, whereas Kramer and Specht (1975) and Mann (1978) have explored organisational and planning models. One model with considerable potential for the understanding of community processes within contexts such as tourism development is that known as social representations. This perspective was first advanced in psychology by Wundt in 1879 (Farr 1984), but was then taken up by the discipline of sociology by Durkheim, and developed into his theory generally known as 'representations collectivities'. The French psychologist Moscovici reintroduced this perspective to psychology during the 1960s with his study of psychoanalysis within French society. Since that time various psychologists such as Farr and Moscovici (1984) have explored the notions underlying social representations in a wide variety of applied psychology contexts.

One of the most fundamental perspectives within this theoretical formulation is the idea of the community and community-level perceptions and ways of thinking. As such, this model has perspectives sympathetic to various domains within psychology (e.g. cognitive, social and clinical) but has the potential to make a unique contribution to understanding within community psychology. Basically, Moscovici (1973) would define social representations as more than opinions, images and attitudes about some prominent social reality. Social representations are systems of thinking shared by large numbers of community members and the ways in which they order community reality and provide codes or language to facilitate social exchange. They are shared thought-forms and language by which community members can classify unambiguously the various aspects of their world and community history (see Farr, 1978, Moscovici, 1973, Pearce, Moscardo and Ross, 1996).

It is argued that the understanding of tourism and its social impacts may be assisted by reference to this set of ideas. It may be that tourists and tourist impacts are comprehended by host community members by way of certain social representations. It is possible that there are a circumscribed number of overarching or fundamental representations by which community members regard tourist impacts as beneficial or detrimental, and that these characterisations typify and channel their social judgements. There is now some evidence from media reports, letters to the editor columns and talk-back radio programs to suggest that tourists are perceived as either overwhelmingly destructive 'terrorists' or economically beneficial 'goldmines' (Lim 1988; MacKay-Payne 1988). Pearce (1990) has referred to these widespread characteristics as 'the green' and 'the gold' reactions to tourist development. Thus it is possible that these particular reactions to tourists and tourism constitute social representations that symbolise fundamental community processes and therefore provide an insight into how a host community orders its social life in a positive and advantageous fashion.

Perhaps one of the most important notions associated with an understanding of tourism's specific impacts within a community psychology framework is that of perception of community well-being. The study of constituents of an individual's perception of community well-being has been the subject of considerable interest (Galster and Hesser 1981; Miller 1980). Earlier understandings of community functioning were founded on traditional indicators such as rates of employment, education and crime. However, the quality of community life cannot be fully comprehended without an understanding of the individual's subjective evaluation of a range of elements such as services and facilities. Allen and Beattie (1984) argue that an individual's subjective evaluation of services, opportunities and attributes in a community are better predictors of overall perceptions of the quality of community life than the more traditional orthodox measures. They have revealed that the perceptions of economic and social dimensions are important in the prediction of overall satisfaction with community life.

Yet even from a subjective perspective, the analysis of community life has been restricted by a lack of agreement over those aspects of community life which are appropriate indicators of satisfaction within that community. Some researchers have concentrated on services offered in a community (Murdoch and Schriner 1979; Christenson 1976). They would hold that residents' overall satisfaction with community services is a good predictor of overall community life satisfaction. Other commentators have emphasised that social and environmental factors must be included in a complete understanding of community life and functioning. Opportunities to foster relationships with friends, community cohesiveness, group decision-making, open spaces, climate, and topography have been suggested as factors which contribute to a resident's overall assessment regarding the well-being of community life (Ladewig and McCann 1980; Flanaghan 1978; Goudy 1977). While there is no clear agreement as to what are the fundamental constituents which make up this notion of community functioning, there is little doubt that satisfied community members make for happier tourist destinations.

The variety of impact

It is a truism but nonetheless important to state that local resident responses to tourism development and impacts have been extensively studied over the last decade or so (Belisle and Hoy 1980; Brougham and Butler 1977; Cooke 1982; Lui and Var 1984; Lui, Sheldon and Var 1987; Murphy 1981; 1983; Pizam 1978; Ross 1989; Rothman 1978; and Thomason, Crompton and Kamp 1979). In summary, these studies have focused on how various residents differ in their reactions to the impacts of tourism on community life. Studies by Lui and Var (1986), Var, Kendall and Tarakcioglu (1985) and Pizam (1978) have investigated a variety of socio-demographic characteristics among residents in their reactions to tourist impacts. Belisle and Hoy (1980), Pizam (1978) and Sheldon and Var (1984) have found that the perceived impacts of tourism decrease as the distance between residents' homes and the tourist zone increases. Murphy (1981, 1983), and Thomason, Crompton and Kamp (1979) have found that positive attitudes towards tourism's impacts on a community increase along with an individual's economic dependency on tourism.

Perceived environmental impacts

Resident perceptions of the environmental impacts of tourism are now becoming an important field of study in various parts of the world. Lui, Sheldon and Var (1987) have made the point that regional resident perceptions of tourism vary in quality and intensity. Farrell (1979) discusses differences between 'western' versus 'pacific' thinking on this subject, as well as 'island' versus 'continental' approaches in understanding the perceived environmental impacts of tourism. Lui et al. (1987) have found differences between residents of Hawaii and North Wales and Turkey in regard to the estimated physical impacts of tourism. Residents' perceptions of tourism's environmental impacts have also been found to be a function of the tourist-resident ratio, and related to the carrying capacity of the area. Lui et al. (1987) argue that as the ratio of tourists-to-residents increases, so too does the perception of negative impact on the physical environment, as does the corresponding need to protect what remains of the environment. Pizam (1982) has found that high concentrations of tourists were associated with strong concerns about the physical environment. Duffield and Long (1982) have found that those regions enjoying a low tourist-resident ratio tended to have residents who were positive about the effects of tourism. Finally, Belisle and Hoy (1980) concluded that positive resident attitudes are a function of the stage of tourist development of the area, and therefore the perception of the social, cultural and physical impacts of tourism on the community and its environment.

Specific impacts of tourism

Kendall and Var (1984) summarise the research on negative impacts as revealing concerns which impinge upon residents' lifestyle such as crowding, traffic congestion, noise, litter, property destruction, pollution, alterations to community appearances, destruction of wildlife, and ad hoc development; Travis (1982), in similar vein, cites damage to cultural resources, land use loss, and increased urbanisation. Both Cohen (1978) and Pigram (1980) have written about the potential destruction of the physical environment as the result of tourism development. The following positive impacts of tourism have been adumbrated in the literature: more and better leisure facilities, more developed beaches and parks, and greater recognition of the importance of conserving historical buildings.

In a landmark study of both the negative and positive responses of residents to the impacts of tourism, Lui, Sheldon and Var (1987) examined factors related to environmental protection, economic benefits, social costs and cultural benefits. They examined these factors in three very different contexts: Hawaii, North Wales and Istanbul. They found that the impact of tourism on the physical environment is of universal concern, and that both Hawaiian and Welsh residents rank environmental protection as being of paramount concern, compared with other social and economic effects. The study also revealed some situation-specific concerns: in Hawaii and Wales, where tourism is a significant part of the economy, residents were primarily concerned with the negative impact on their environment. The Welsh also evinced a concern over the purchase of property by foreigners. In contrast they found that in Turkey, which hopes to expand its tourist industry, residents were concerned with the development of facilities, hospitality, and promotion of the area. Lui, Sheldon and Var (1987) also found that residents did not only blame tourists for environmental changes, but that they also comprehended many of the benefits brought about by the industry, such as the preservation of historic buildings and precincts. They concluded from a comparison of the three locations that residents in more touristically developed regions may be more aware of both positive and negative impacts largely because tourism is kept to the forefront of thinking through media debates on public issues, community discussions, and the witnessing of frequent large-scale tourism development.

Allen, Long, Perdue and Keiselbach (1988) investigated a set of some 33 specific elements of community life which represent seven aspects of community functioning: public services, economic factors, environmental factors, medical services, citizen involvement, formal education and recreational services, along with tourist development. Their study revealed that citizen involvement, public services and environment were the most sensitive to tourism development. They suggest that as tourism development increases, respondents' satisfaction with opportunities for citizen involvement and public services declines, along with the importance that residents attach to citizen involvement. They also suggest that satisfaction with medical services and recreational opportunities along with the importance placed on environmental issues are more a function of population size than overall tourism development.

In addressing a US situation which might also be applicable to a number of single-industry cities and towns in Australia, Kent (1977) refers to the tourism industry in Hawaii as a new kind of sugar. He tells how Hawaii's tourism industry is closely controlled by a few major companies. Here every effort is made to ensure that tourists use their facilities, leaving little spillage for the small-scale and local operator. Kent (1977) makes the point that in

Hawaii there has been virtually no socio-economic development of benefit to the locals, and that the old industries and values have been replaced by a modern equivalent. Such a situation cannot but be accompanied by a degree of animosity on the part of the residents.

Tourism-community issues are said to be of major importance now by many international commentators. One of the major tourism planning and research issues over the past decade or so has been the equivocal and sometimes conflicting evidence revealed from the growing number of studies of resident-visitor relationships in various contexts around the world. Studies based largely in underdeveloped regions have revealed an association between large-scale commercial tourist development and perceived deteriorating social conditions in the host communities. Evidence for this resident-visitor alienation has been found in contexts such as Hawaii (Farrell 1979; Finney 1977; Lui, Sheldon and Var 1987), the Caribbean (Pollard 1976; Rivers 1973), and the Mediterranean (Rudney 1980; Pi-Sunyer 1978). Such contexts have emerged as major tourist destinations for European and North American visitors. Yet not all studies yield this resident-visitor hostility effect. Boissevan (1977) found that many of the residents of Malta saw positive benefits flowing from the development accompanying tourism. Moreover, positive findings have been found by Andressen and Murphy (1986) in Canada, by Cant (1980) in New Zealand and by Rothman (1978), and Thomason, Crompton and Kamp (1979) in various United States contexts. It thus appears that the reaction of residents to visitors is by no means uniform and may be related to a variety of unique local factors. Thus this situation parallels that outlined by Lui *et al.* (1987) where concerns about community changes vary markedly across the tourist world.

Critical issues determining resident attitudes

In the US, Smith (1980) has proposed a model to account for spatial effects. She argues that if visitor expectations and needs can be met in a core tourism zone, then the visitors will seldom need to leave the area and stray into adjacent residential neighbourhoods. This assists in retaining the privacy of the local residents. If, however, the core zone becomes inadequate in some way, she maintains that development in the adjacent residential areas is likely to result. Direct and negative contact between tourists and locals are said to be likely to occur. Smith's model posits as a general principle that those who live further from the current core zone will be more likely to avoid personal contact with tourists if they so desire, even though they may be benefiting economically either directly or indirectly from tourism. Murphy (1980, 1981) has found that certain types of residents have developed much more positive attitudes to tourism than have others. Those residents with a commercial interest in tourism were found more likely to be favourably disposed to the tourist than were other residents. Those who own or operate businesses and those who work in those businesses have been found to be more likely to have prominent and positive attitudes to tourism than those who have no direct involvement or perceive that they derive no benefit from tourists. Murphy (1980) in a study of three English tourist centres, found that the decision-making groups in the communities, represented by the business sector and local administration had a more positive attitude to tourism than the other residents. Pizam (1978, 1980) in a study centred on Cape Cod, Massachusetts, found that businessmen saw tourism as having a greater positive impact on the quality of life of the district than did other residents, and that they also attributed better police, more fire protection and more recreational facilities to the presence of tourism.

Murphy (1981) has found a strong link between the relative seasonal importance of tourism to the community and resident attitudes. For the English tourist centre of Torquay, tourism dominates the life of the city, and there is a marked seasonal variation. Here residents were divided between those who were strongly in favour and those who were highly critical. Those who were highly critical of tourism referred to the domination of the city by the industry and the seasonality of employment. In contrast, Murphy notes that the more balanced economies of cities such as York and Windsor provided a less conspicuous industry, which generated less emotional responses and more moderate attitudes.

Murphy has also made the point that community attitudes are related to the growth stage of the industry and its concomitant volume of business. He posits that as the industry grows in a centre, not only does the quality of social interaction change, but residents come under increasing pressure as they compete for limited space and resources within their home environment. Murphy has found that the most frequently quoted irritant for residents is congestion: in local restaurants and hotels, longer shopping lines and traffic and parking. Other concerns focus upon issues such as community development appearing to take place to suit the tourist developers and not residents, concerns that property values will be inflated and that rates and taxes will be increased by local councils so as to raise more money for investment in tourist infrastructure. Murphy has also found that locals were concerned about the growth of litter and vandalism which they commonly associated with the influx of tourists. He concludes that if the industry is to improve its image and profile within local communities, it must find ways to enhance the advantages of the industry and minimise the problems. He believes that an appropriate place to start is by reducing the social stress and irritants associated with increasing business volume by way of separating functions and placing limits on development in particular zones.

Host community stress

It is of considerable importance to take into account the functioning of the host community in any understudy of the tourism phenomenon. The emergence of obvious negative community attitudes towards the industry and tourists has led to the proposal of several visitor-resident models within the social sciences which attempt to incorporate both the abovementioned positive and negative components. Doxey (1975) has proposed the 'Irridex Model' which seeks to identify and explain the cumulative effects of tourism development over time on social relationships. This commentator has developed a model that postulates a direct link between increased community irritation or stress, and continual tourism development. It suggests that in the early stages of development tourists are likely to be greeted with enthusiasm by local residents. This new industry is perceived to bring enjoyment and revenue, and the earlier tourists are seen to be interested in and appreciative of local customs and lifestyles. As the volume of tourists increases, contact between residents and visitors becomes less personal and more commercialised, and visitors are seen to demand more facilities built specifically for them. At this stage the tourist industry is no longer new or a novelty, but rather taken for granted in the life of the city. Local people are said to develop a more apathetic attitude to the industry.

If development continues, it may exceed community tolerance thresholds because of such factors as increased congestion, rising prices and changes to customary ways of life. Moreover, residents may feel that their community is being greatly altered and they've not been consulted about this. Here the costs of accommodating the tourist industry are perceived as beginning to exceed benefits. This annoyance can change to antagonism if tourism and its facilities are perceived to be the origin of the locals' economic and social problems. Doxey here cites the instances of murder of wealthy white tourists in some lesser-developed countries. However, many other less noticeable instances may be found.

Some commentators such as Belisle and Hoy (1980) are said to have evidence in support of Doxey's model. However, Murphy (1985), commenting on the limitations of Doxey's model, has pointed out that the model suggests a unidirectional sequence, where residents' attitudes and reactions will change over time and within a predictable sequence. He believes that visitor reactions to the tourism industry are often more complex than this, and that Butler's (1980) model cited by Murphy (1985) is somewhat more adequate in this context. Butler has advanced a model which has been founded on the product life cycle concept. In this concept, sales of a product are said to proceed slowly at first, are then said to experience a rapid rate of growth, stabilise, and finally, often decline. Tourists initially are said to come to an area in relatively small numbers. As facilities are provided and the destination becomes better known, numbers of tourists increase. With further promotion and the growth of facilities, the venue's popularity is said to escalate rapidly. However, the rate of increase is said to decline at the point where limits of carrying capacity are achieved. Butler argues that at this point the attractiveness of an area declines vis à vis other tourist areas because of overuse and the general impact of tourists. At this point the number of visitors may actually start to decline. Butler is thus advancing a stage model; e.g. exploration, involvement, development, consolidation, stagnation, decline or rejuvenation. It is worthwhile noting here that Butler's (1980) model is more flexible and less deterministic than the Doxey model. This is particularly evident at the stagnation stage where an area may choose either to rejuvenate or decline, depending upon the circumstances prevailing within the location at that time. As such, Butler's model would seem to be much more adequate in encompassing the various reactions of destinations to the growth of tourism.

Butler (1980) cited by Murphy (1985) has identified two groups of factors that can influence visitor-resident relationships. First of all, the characteristics of visitors is said to have an impact that extends beyond the physical impact of increasing numbers. Butler argues that the tourists' length of stay and their racial and economic characteristics need to be considered as well as their numbers. As well, a destination's own characteristics, it is said, will help determine its ability to absorb the growing number of visitors. Characteristics such as its level of economic development, the spatial distribution of its tourist focus in relation to other economic activities, the strength of its local culture, and local political and community attitudes, it is said, will affect visitor-resident relationships. Butler makes the point that large metropolitan areas, with their tourists largely concentrated in and around a core zone, are able to handle millions of tourists, whereas small rural settlements may have trouble handling a few thousand visitors.

Methodological issues

An examination of the host-visitor literature reveals a complex set of measurement approaches and research designs in the understanding of community reactions to tourists. Many researchers employ the survey method and present questions related to economic, environmental, social or cultural issues. Residents are usually invited to participate within a Likert framework. It is the case that relatively little research has been done authenticating this procedure in the particular context. A few studies, however, have begun the process of exploring these issues.

Maddox (1985) has investigated the validity of several frequently employed satisfaction scales within tourism in Nova Scotia. He examined graphic scales, Likert-type scales, and faces scales portraying moods. He reports that while all measures performed well, the delighted-terrible scale appeared to be superior on various measures of validity. He cites Um and Crompton (1987) as arguing that one of the most notable yet neglected variables involved in tourist-host research is that of residents' attachment levels to their community. They have derived a measure for this concept which includes years of residence, birthplace and heritage, and argue that the Guttman Scale so formed is a useful instrument in distinguishing between recent and long-established or 'native' residents' perceptions of tourism impacts on the community.

Allen, Long, Perdue and Kieselbach (1988) have argued that it is essential to understand host-visitor relationships within the contexts of tourist development level and community life satisfaction. They would argue that the level of tourism development a community has experienced, together with residents' perceptions of community life are essential to the comprehension of community reactions to tourism and tourists. In exploring the concept of tourism development level, they postulate the notion of optimum carrying capacity for any community, and cite various factors in the measurement of this, such as physical accommodation, tourist density and tourist-related scales. They opt for a measure of tourist development which represents the ratio of lodging, eating and drinking establishments sales to the community's gross sales receipts. They admit that there are problems associated with this and indeed any measure of tourist development, and have opted for a measure that was consistently available in any community. They do, however, admit that such a measure is not without some problems (i.e. underestimation).

Perhaps Allen et al.'s most useful contribution in the measurement of host-visitor relationships is in the area of community values. They have argued that, in order to understand community reactions to tourism, it is necessary to comprehend which particular facilities and attributes of a community are seen as most notable and satisfying. To this end they have refined and made specific a list of 33 elements of community life, and concluded that there is a significant relationship between a number of these elements (such as potential citizen involvement in community affairs, public services and the physical environment), and level of tourism development in various North American communities. Thus an inclusion of potentially notable and specific elements of community life has been found to be useful in the understanding of how communities react to tourism. It may be that those particular community attributes which are seen to be vital in the community's life and perceived as being altered by tourist development are the most useful predictors of negative responses to tourism.

Impacts and community services

A social impacts and community services study of tourism has been conducted in the Far Northern Queensland region, which includes the tourist city of Cairns (Ross 1990a, 1990b, 1991b, 1992). A set of thirty community facilities similar to those employed by Allen *et al.* (1988) were included in a survey schedule, together with items measuring global assessments of tourism's positive and negative impacts on the individual and the community, and an assessment of enjoyment levels at living in that community. Items rated as most negatively affected were: cost of buying land, cost of buying a house, cost of renting a house, cost of living and crime levels. Items rated as most positively affected were: hotels and restaurants, shopping facilities, business opportunities, parks and gardens, and entertainment facilities. Those items with more neutral ratings (i.e. not affected by tourism) were: fire-fighting services, general appearance of respondent's street, friendliness of local residents, emergency health services, and general appearance of the city.

Respondents were also requested to rate the five most important community services and facilities for them. These emerged as: cost of buying land, cost of buying a house, job opportunities, scenic beauty of the area, and medical services. Cost of buying land and cost of buying a house already appear among the negative impacts; job opportunities was rated as a positive impact and thus has been added to the positive impacts, for the purposes of analysis; whereas scenic beauty and medical services were neutrally rated and thus added to the neutral impacts list. Respondents in this study also rated the extent to which they enjoyed living in this community. Results suggest low overall levels of association between these variables with the highest association between levels of community enjoyment and personal negative impacts accounting for only 22% of the variability. However, standardised deviation scores suggest that the personal impacts, positive and negative, revealed a respective heightened and lessened likelihood of presence along with enjoyment than would be expected under an assumption of independence between these variables.

Further analyses involved sub-groups in the population thought to be more vulnerable or sensitive to the negative impacts of tourist development in a host community — the older residents and the longer-term residents. These revealed significant correlations between lower levels of community enjoyment and time-focused impact judgements. These negative perceptions were prominent for older and longer-term residents who believed that tourism's negative impacts would become more severe in three years time, and who desired a reduction in this tourism development for their area. While some of these analyses are based on relatively small numbers, they do provide some evidence to suggest that members of this particular group do have heightened forebodings about the future, expressed as strong wishes regarding the reduction in tourism development for their community. These findings may, at least, suggest that this particular group of residents is particularly sensitive to tourist development or perceive that they in particular have little to gain and much to lose within the context of tourism development in their residential area. Such findings do, at least, deserve further research scrutiny.

This study has identified those community services and facilities rated by residents as being positively and negatively influenced by tourism development. This community has also rated a number of services and facilities as being relatively unchanged by the growth of tourism in their city. Positive effects focused on the leisure and entertainment domains together with greater financial opportunities that tourism was deemed to attract. Negative effects involved perceptions of escalating living costs involving major household expenditure items for most families: land, houses or rental accommodation. A safety concern was also registered here, with crime levels being seen to rise as the result of tourism development. The major community facilities deemed to be unaffected by tourism involved local government services such as fire-fighting and emergency health, as well as the general appearance of the street and the area and the general cohesiveness of the community in the form of the friendliness of the local residents. Thus while positive impacts revolved around leisure and economic opportunities, negative impacts principally involved increased costs of accommodation, while neutral impacts involved lack of change in basic community services provided by local government agencies, together with social and interpersonal impacts concerning a continuance of the friendliness of the local residents.

Residents of this tourist community clearly judged the impacts of this dominant industry to be more serious at the individual rather than the community level. Individual negative impacts were much more likely to be associated with judgements of lower levels of community functioning than were overall community negative impact judgements, leading to the conclusion that it is not the overall perceived impacts within a community but rather the personal nature of the overall impact judgement that will be associated with a diminution of community satisfaction as perceived by the residents.

Tourism development on Cyprus — Residents' attitudes

Akis, Peristianis and Warner (1996) have sought to examine the perceptions of both Greek and Turkish Cypriot residents in regard to coastal tourism development. In particular they have investigated Butler's (1980) hypothesis regarding an inverse relationship between the level of tourism development and perceived negative impacts on the social, economic and environmental attributes of a host community, as this hypothesis may apply to tourism communities on Cyprus. Akis *et al.* largely confirm the general applicability of Butler's (1980) hypothesis, though suggest that a significant proportion of uncertain responses received from residents in less developed areas may point to the need for some modification of the hypothesis in specific circumstances.

Akis *et al.* note that one aspect of the hypothesis, that of friendliness, has produced some interesting results in this study. They report that as tourism grows, and thus as interactions between tourists and residents increase, they expected Cypriots to show more resentment and hostility to visitors. However, they found that, at all three locations, those who have more exposure to tourists were found to regard interactions with them as positive. Indeed they report that as frequency of contact with tourists increases, the proportion of respondents seeing the contacts as positive also increases. Akis *et al.* believe that the reason for the difference that residents exhibit between their perceptions of the benefits of tourism and their perceptions of the quality of their interactions with tourists might well be explained by the fact that the distinction between the level of tourism development and the number of tourists is not clearly explained in the literature. It is possible, they say, that as general tourism development increases, residents' positive views of tourism decline, whereas, as the number of tourists increases, positive views of these tourists as individuals might also increase.

Akis *et al.* go on to make the point that it would be valuable to find a way to 'decouple' the link between increases in tourist numbers and proliferation of infrastructure. Here they are suggesting ways be found to sever the apparent link between increasing numbers of people and increasing numbers of hotels, restaurants, etc., so that a destination might be able to enjoy growth in numbers without any of the concomitant perceived negative impacts of development. They suggest that some ways that this aim may be advanced might include the extension of visitor seasons or the dispersal of visitors over a wider area. They conclude that while this suggested 'decoupling' may have its costs which ought to be taken into consideration, nonetheless the process should be explored further so that the perceived negative effects of tourism development may be ameliorated in host communities such as those on Cyprus.

Summary

This chapter has introduced some of the central concepts and studies associated with the social impacts of tourism. The chapter has presented some of the major positive and negative factors associated with tourist growth in any host community. The chapter has also presented results from studies in rapidly growing tourism communities.

CHAPTER 9 **DISCUSSION TOPICS**

How might social representations theory be employed in the comprehension of the social impacts of tourism?

Outline major factors which seem to influence resident reactions.

Discuss the adequacy of Doxey's model of impact.

Describe major measurement procedures employed in social impact studies.

How might the link between increasing tourist numbers and greater tourism development be severed so that host communities positively regard visitors?

10

A Summary Model of Tourist Behaviour

LEARNING OBJECTIVES

An understanding of:

- The value of a social network theory in drawing together a range of tourism/psychology topics.
- Methodological requirements in the exploration of social networks within the tourism domain.
- Current research questions generated by this perspective.

E ach of the previous chapters has concentrated on one particular topic from the Psychology and Tourism domain. These chapters have explored both the theory and application of major ideas as well as their exploration in a variety of international contexts. This final chapter will now present a set of overarching theoretical perspectives, methodological options, and future research and application possibilities which draw together many of the seemingly disparate topics of psychology and tourism. The chapter offers a higher-order model that may generate and direct a range of future research projects within this synthesis. The social network perspective is presented in this concluding chapter as a useful synthesising conceptualisation. The basic tenets are presented, as are a number of the implications for tourism research, including possible future research directions energised by this approach. The chapter then concludes with an overall assessment of the present state of learning within the psychology of tourism domain, together with some comments regarding the short and medium term impact of this area in both the academic and industry contexts.

A social network perspective

Stokowski (1990) has advanced a Social Network perspective so as to conceptualise tourism. Stokowski has made the point that, although social networks research has received considerable attention as an emerging scientific paradigm in a variety of other disciplines, it has yet to be developed fully in tourism research. Stokowski argues that the notion of a network of people connected through social relationships provides the basis for network analytic techniques. Social network analysis is said to be a set of methods for mapping the simultaneous interactions of multiple actors involved in interpersonal relationships and then analysing the structural patterns and regularities that make up the network of relationships. Stokowski points out that in mapping these social networks, individuals or corporate actors are described as nodes and the relational ties between them as links. She suggests that a network is basically a composite pattern of actual and potential relational linkages that exist among a defined set or system of nodes. Stokowski argues that the matrix of social relationships is not always symmetric, not always chosen voluntarily, and sometimes not even visible to those persons outside the relation. Moreover, she points out that the social network perspective suggests that people live in worlds of potentially expansive and diverse social connections. The psychological task is to determine how multiple social relationships are arranged and ordered and what the patterns mean for such phenomena as recreation behaviours. For Stokowski, conducting a network analysis requires that researchers focus attention on several issues that generally are not problematic in traditional recreation research such as the nature of social relationships, specification of the network boundaries, the procedures of network sampling, and measurement of network structures.

Two types of social network analysis are said to be common: the study of egocentric networks and the study of total social networks (Stokowski, 1990). Regardless of the type of network under study, the data collected are, according to Stokowski (1990), sociometric in nature. Questions are asked about a social actor's interpersonal relationships, exchanges, activities, and communication with other entities. She points out that these data have traditionally been gathered by means of observational and interview techniques or survey research methods. Data collection and analyses are said to pose special problems for social network analysts. An understanding of what subjects mean by the relational terms they use is cited as one such problem. Individuals assign meanings to interpersonal relations on the basis of various criteria. According to Stokowski, there is still substantial work to be done on specifying relational criteria for network analysis and on determining whether reported contents are comparable.

Measuring network structures

Stokowski (1990) has pointed out that in social network analysis, the focus of study is the interactional properties of relational linkages, the arrangement of nodes in relation to one another, and the structural characteristics of network systems. Stokowski believes that there are several interactional and structural properties that may be employed to measure network structures. Table 10.1 lists and defines some of the most commonly used concepts. In Table 10.1 interactional criteria refer to different aspects of specific relationships, and structural criteria refer to the nature of the network as a whole. Stokowski points out that these concepts are not all utilised in every study but are differentially utilised to analyse specific aspects of the relational or structural characteristics of social networks. It is also pointed out that the operationalisation of concepts is not always consistent across disciplines, but there is now a diverse literature about social networks to guide investigators on the proper application of concepts.

Social networks and tourism

To be meaningful for tourism research, Stokowski (1990) believes that the social network approach should be theoretically grounded in two ways. First, there is said to be a need to specify how specific types of relational commitments underpin particular kinds of tourist behaviours. Of all types of community network relationships she poses the question as to which ties are the most productive and meaningful for tourism. Second, a theory about the structural consequences of tourism relationships must, according to Stokowski, be constructed. Whereas social groups research begins and ends with individuals arranged in bounded groups at tourism sites, social network analysis must, according to Stokowski, consider how tourism ties have broader implications in day-to-day community life. Assuming that some social relationships are more important than others for tourism behaviour, she believes that the next step is to describe how these significant relationships are ordered in broader, extended networks of the community and to hypothesise about the meaning of networks for behaviour. As yet, these issues are said to remain largely unaddressed in tourism research.

In encouraging and developing social networks research in tourism, Stokowski (1990) has also pointed out that there are at least three general research areas that must be considered. First, is said to be the analysis concerned with how community social relationships promote varied social involvements and groupings at tourism places for leisure purposes. This is said to ground the analysis of social groups at tourism places in the context of community, where social relationships originate. In addition, this perspective is said to consider the role of both strong and weak social ties in tourism involvement.

Table 10.1   Social Network concepts which may be applied to tourism/hospitality research

Type	Definition
Interactional Criteria	
Frequency	Number and continuity of interactions communication over time
Contents of ties	Purpose and functions of relation, types of relational tie (exchange, obligation, sentiment, power)
Multiplexity	Redundancy of relationships; how many contents are combined in a specific relation
Reciprocity	Degree of symmetry in relation (if A chooses B, does B choose A?)
Strength of ties (strong, weak)	Relative measure of time, affect, intensity, mutuality.
Structural Criteria	
Size	Number of persons or relations in a defined network
Density	Connectedness of network; actual links computed as a proportion of total possible links
Distance or Proximity	Number of links between any two nodes in proximity network
Centrality	Adjacency and influence of nodes and sub-groups in network
Clustering	Partition of ties into network subgroups and cliques
Network roles	
1. Isolate	Peripheral node in a network
2. Bridge	Group member who provides a link to another network subgroup
3. Liaison	Node that links several groups without being a member of any
4. Star	Node with the largest number of communication links
Personal Criteria	
Personality	Personality attribute configurations brought to interactions by individuals

Adapted from Stokowski (1990)

It is suggested that by Stokowski that networks research in this area might study whether and why different types of personal relationships (close or distant) result in different levels of tourism activity commitment; whether network size influences participation in specific tourism activities; how people use networks to gain access to tourism information, resources, and opportunity; and whether involvement in highly connected social networks provides individuals with more tourism opportunities and satisfactions than involvement in less dense networks.

Stokowski believes that a second area of important research is the analysis of how individuals and social groups interact in structuring on-site tourism activities and social meanings during the tourism experience. Equivalent to the on-site stage of the recreation experience, this topic is said to broaden the study of social groups to question how interactions occur in and between groups during tourism activities. She urges that research in this area might thus study how information is disseminated across the on-site network among groups of tourists involved in activities, whether the presence or absence of specific others (significant or non-significant others, experts or non-experts, network isolates or stars) influences behaviours in tourism settings, how solitary tourists create and present network affiliations in an effort to enhance or limit interactions with others during tourism activities, and how tourists differentially utilise host community networks to increase control and satisfaction during the recreation experience.

Finally, Stokowski believes there is a need to study how relationships activated in the context of tourism influence subsequent community social network relationships. In terms of the tourism experience, this issue is said to focus on post-activity network interactions and involvements during the return travel and recollection stages. It also is said to acknowledge the potentially long-term effects of social relationships developed during tourism experiences on future tourism and community action. Finally, it is said to suggest that behaviour in one social context is, to some extent, dependent on behaviour in other contexts. Stokowski points out that important research questions in this area might include analysis of the extent to which shared tourism activity participation produces further obligations for community social involvements; how conflict in one area of a tourism network influences subsequent social and recreational involvements with close, and more distant, others; how community networks are manipulated for personal interest; and, whether or to what extent, tourism network ties offer unique resources to people.

The Stokowski model also facilitates the posing of research questions emanating from the various domains of psychology of tourism as examined in this book. Issues such as the motivation of tourism behaviour may be influenced by the type, destinations or proximity of social networks, either while on holidays or before commencing the holiday, depending on a particular tourist activity. Basic personality dimensions may have a major influence upon the particular tourism networks in which travellers become enmeshed. Moreover, fundamental attitudes to issues such as the physical or social environment may be mediated or tempered by the constantly changing networks that surround travellers. Such questions are worth exploring in regard to individual tourists.

Further research questions may be posed in respect of social networks and domains such as the social impacts of tourism on host communities or human resource management and the tourism/hospitality industry. How, for example, could a change in network structure or international style provide a wider perception of empowerment to a host community currently experiencing general feelings of being swamped by tourists and tourism development? Do tourism/hospitality industry worker networks of various types and patterns facilitate more affiliations among employees and accompanying higher levels of work satisfaction? Which are the tourism networks that promote optimum levels of positive post-visit evaluations and thus widespread word-of-mouth recommendations to potential visitors? The network perspective opens up the possibility of an exploration of these questions.

Summary

The various studies reported in this book suggest that the understanding of tourism from a psychological perspective has advanced considerably in the last few decades. In the 1960s relatively little had been achieved in this area. Moreover, at that time most psychologists were either not aware of or not interested in the application of psychological knowledge and methodology to the understanding of tourism. However, this is not now the case, particularly in a number of contexts such as Europe, North America and Australasia, which have in recent times come to the greater realisation that tourism is a major and growing industry, increasingly essential for the economic well-being of many citizens. Psychological research in the tourism field is now increasingly sophisticated methodologically as well as conceptually diverse.

Future research opportunities may lie in a number of basic directions. First, there is now an awareness of the need for descriptive studies to precede and comprehend the social phenomena involved, before complex empirical experimentation is initiated. Such an awareness is justified on the grounds that any relatively new or relatively poorly comprehended tourism phenomenon is best approached in this way, lest formal experimental investigation miss or fail to comprehend fundamental elements of it in a procrustean rush to document its dimensions. Second, and perhaps paradoxically, there is now the desire to generate meta-models or overarching conceptualisations so that the diversity of tourism psychology can be more fully integrated, and not merely be presented as a set of seemingly disparate topics such as motivation, attitudes, personality, etc. The social network model may be seen in such a light, and represents the efforts of members of a discipline to seek coherence and the greater predictability that this is regarded as bringing. One of the challenges ahead for those active in the tourism/psychology arena would seem to be an accommodation and reconciliation of these two apparently contradictory research directions. The ways in which this dilemma is solved will be of considerable importance because they will either open up new avenues of understanding or channel much effort into unproductive disputation. The vigorous, positive and creative efforts thus far displayed in this arena would suggest that the former will prevail.

CHAPTER 10   DISCUSSION TOPICS

Describe the basic units of analysis within the social network approach.

In which ways are network structures explored?

Provide an example of how social network research might illuminate tourist behaviour.

Examine the process of constructing meta-models in the interpretation of current research findings within the psychology of tourism field.

References

Adams, D. (1954). *The Anatomy of Personality.* New York: Doubleday.

Ahmed, S. (1986). Understanding residents' reactions to tourism marketing strategies. *Journal of Travel Research, 25,* 13-18.

Airey, D. & Frontistis, A. (1997). Attitudes to careers in tourism: an Anglo-Greek comparison. *Tourism Management, 18,* 149-158.

Ajzen, E., & Fishbein, M. (1980). *Understanding Attitudes and Predicting Social Behaviour.* Englewood Cliffs, NJ: Prentice-Hall.

Akis, S., Peristianis, N. & Warner, J. (1996). Residents attitudes to tourism development: The case of Cyprus. *Tourism Management, 17,* 481-494.

Allen, L.R. & Beattie, R. (1984). The role of leisure as an indicator of overall satisfaction with community life. *Journal of Leisure Research, 16,* 99-109.

Allen, L.R., Long, P.T., Perdue, R.R. & Kieselbach, S. (1988). The impact of tourism development on residents' perceptions of community life. *Journal of Travel Research, 27,* 16-21.

Allport, G. (1937). *Personality, A Psychological Interpretation.* New York: HRW.

Anderssen, P. & Colberg, R. (1973). Multivariate analysis in travel research: A tool for travel package design and market segmentation. *The Travel Research Association: Fourth Annual Conference Proceedings* (pp. 225-240). Sun Valley, ID: Author.

Andressen, B. & Murphy, P.E. (1986). Tourism development in Canadian travel corridors: two surveys of resident attitudes. *World Leisure and Recreation, October,* 17-22.

Ankomah, P.K. & Crompton, J.L. (1992). Tourism cognitive distance. *Annals of Tourism Research, 19,* 323-343.

Appleyard, D. (1970). Styles and methods of structuring a city. *Environment and Behaviour, 2,* 100-117.

Argyle, M., Furnham, A. & Graham, J.A. (1981). *Social Situations.* Cambridge: Cambridge University Press.

Ashworth, G.J. (1985). *Resident Reactions to Tourism in Norwich and Great Yarmouth.* Groningen: Geographical Institute, University of Groningen, The Netherlands.

Assael, H. (1984). *Consumer Behaviour and Marketing Action.* Boston: Kent.

Atkinson, J.W. (1958). *Motivators in Fantasy, Action and Society.* New York: Oxford University Press.

Atkinson, J.W. (1964). *An Introduction to Motivation.* Princetown, N.J.: Van Nostrand.

Atkinson, J.W. & Birch D. (1970). *The Dynamics of Action.* New York: Wiley.

Atkinson, J.W. & Birch, D. (1978). *An Introduction to Motivation.* New York: Van Nostrand.

Atlas, J. (1984). Beyond Demographics: How Madison Avenue knows who you are and what you want. *The Atlantic, 254 (October),* 49-58.

Ayer, A.J. (1959). Privacy. *Proceedings of the British Academy, 45,* 43-65.

Babbie, E. (1992). *The Practice of Social Research.* Belmont, Calif: Wadsworth.

Bailly, A.S. (1986). Subjective distance and spatial representations. *Geoforum, 1,* 81-88.

Bandura, A. (1986). Social Foundations of Thought and Action. Englewood-Cliffs, N.J.: Prentice-Hall.

Banner, D.K. & Himmerfarb, A. (1985). The work/leisure relationship: Toward a useful typology. LODJ, 6 (4), 22-55.

Barnes, J.A. (1954). Class and committees in a Norwegian island parish. Human Relations, 7, 39-58.

Beatty, S.E., Kahle L.R., Homer, P. & Misra, S. (1985). Alternative measurement approaches to consumer values: The list of values and the Rokeach Value Survey. *Psychology and Marketing, 2,* 181-200.

Belisle, F.J. & Hoy, D.R. (1980). The perceived impact of tourism by residents: a case study in Santa Marta, Colombia. *Annals of Tourism Research, 7,* 83-101.

Belk, R.W. (1975). Situational variables and consumer behaviour. *Journal of Consumer Research, 2,* 157-164.

Bell, P.A., Fisher, G.D. & Loomis, R.J. (1981). *Environmental Psychology.* Philadelphia: Saunders.

Bem, D.J. (1967). Self-perception: An alternative interpretation of cognitive dissonance phenomena. *Psychological Review, 74,* 183-200.

Berger, P.L. & H. Kellner (1964). Marriage and the construction of reality. *Diogenes, 46,* 1-24.

Berkowitz, S.D. (1982). *An introduction to structural analysis: The network approach to social research.* Toronto: Butterworth & Co.

Birch, D. & Veroff, J. (1966). *Motivation: A Study of Action.* Monteray, Calif.: Brooks/Cole.

Black, N.L. (1990). A model and methodology to assess changes to heritage buildings. *The Journal of Tourism Studies, 1,* 15-22.

Blau, P.M. (1982). Structural sociology and network analysis. In *Social Structure and Network Analysis.* P.V. Marsden and N. Lin, (Eds). pp. 273-279. Beverly Hills: Sage.

Bott, E. (1955). Urban families: Conjugal roles and social networks. *Human Relations, 8,* 345-384.

Braithwaite, V.A. & Law, H.G. (1985). Structure of human values: Testing the adequacy of the Rokeach Value Survey. *Journal of Personality and Social Psychology, 49,* 250-263.

British Market Research Bureau. (1986). *A Report on the Taking of Farm Holidays in Wales.* London: British Market Research Bureau.

British Tourist Authority. (1975). *Is there 'Welcome' on the Mat?* London: The Economic Intelligence Unit, The British Tourist Authority.

Britton, R.A. (1979). The image of the Third World in tourism marketing. *Annals of Tourism Research, 6,* 318-329.

Brougham, J.E. & Butler, R.W. (1977). *The Social and Cultural Impact of Tourism: A Case Study of Sleat, Isle of Skye.* Edinburgh: Scottish Tourist Board.

Burch, W.R. Jr. (1969). The social circles of leisure: Competing explanations. *Journal of Leisure Research, 1,* 125-147.

Bureau of Tourism Research. (1993). *Australian Tourism Data Card.* Canberra: Bureau of Tourism Research.

Burkart, A.J. & Medlik, S. (1981). *Tourism: Past, Present and Future.* London: Heinemann.

Burt, R.S. (1978). Cohesion versus structural equivalence as a basis for network sub groups. *Sociological Methods and Research, 7,* 189-212.

Burt, R.S. (1981). Studying status/role-sets as ersatz network positions in mass surveys. *Sociological Methods and Research, 9,* 313-337.

Butler, R.W. (1980). The concept of a tourism area cycle of evolution: Implications for management of resources. *Canadian Geographer, 24,* 5-12.

Cadwallader, M.T. (1977). Frame dependence in cognitive maps: An analysis using directional statistics. *Geographical Analysis, 9,* 284-291.

Calatone, R.J., di Benedetto, C.A. & Bojanic D. (1987). A comprehensive review of the tourism forecasting literature. *Journal of Travel Research, 24,* 28-39.

Calatone, R.J., di Benetto, C.A., Hakam, A. & Bojanic, D.C. (1989). Multiple multinational tourism positioning using correspondence analysis. *Journal of Travel Research, 28,* 25-32.

Cameron McNamara. (1986). *Cairns-Mulgrave Tourism Research Study.* Cairns: Cameron McNamara Consultants.

Campbell, J.P., Dunnette, M.D., Lawler, E.E. & Weick, L.E. (1970). *Managerial Behaviour, Performance and Effectiveness.* New York: McGraw-Hill.

Campbell, J.P. & Pritchard, R.D. (1976). Motivation theory in industrial and organizational psychology. In M.D. Dunnette (Eds) *Handbook of Industrial and Organizational Psychology*. Chicago: Rand-McNally.

Cant, G. (1980). The impact of tourism on the host community — the Queenstown example. *New Zealand Man and the Biosphere Report, 6*, 87-97.

Chanowitz, B. & Langer, E. (1980). Knowing more (or less) than you show: understanding control through the mindless-mindfulness distinction. In J. Garber and M.E.P. Seligman (Eds). *Human Helplessness*. New York: Academic Press.

Chon, Kye-Sung. (1987). An assessment of images of Korea as a tourism destination by American tourists. *Hotel and Tourism Management Review, 3*, 155-170.

Chon, Kye-Sung. (1990). The role of destination image in tourism: A review and discussion. *The Tourist Review, 2*, 2-9.

Christenson, J. (1976). Quality of community services: a macro-unidimensional approach with experimental data. *Rural Sociology, 41*, 509-525.

Clawson, M. & Knetsch, J.L. (1966). *Economics of outdoor recreation*. Baltimore: Johns Hopkins University Press.

Clawson, C.J. & Vinson, D.E. (1978). Human values: A historical and interdisciplinary analysis. In *Advances in Consumer Research, Vol 5*, (Ed.). H. Keith Hunt, Ann Arbor, MI: Association for Consumer Research, 396-402.

Cohen, E. (1972). Towards a sociology of international tourism. *Social Research, 39*, 164-82.

Cohen, E. (1973). Nomads from affluence: Notes on the phenomenon of drifter-tourism. *International Journal of Comparative Sociology, 14*, 89-103.

Cohen, E. (1974). Who is a tourist? A conceptual clarification. *Sociological Review, 22*, 527-555.

Cohen, E. (1978). The impact of tourism on the physical environment. *Annals of Tourism Research*, 215-237.

Cohen, E. (1979a). Rethinking the sociology of tourism. *Annals of Tourism Research, 6*, 18-35.

Cohen, E. (1979b). A phenomenology of tourist experiences. *Sociology, 13*, 179-201.

Cohen, E. (1982). Marginal paradises: Bungalow tourism on the islands of Southern Thailand. *Annals of Tourism Research, 9*, 189-228.

Coleman, J., Katz E. & Menzel H. (1957). The diffusion of an innovation among physicians. *Sociometry, 20*, 253-270.

Cook, T.D. & Campbell, D.T. (1976). Design and conduct of quasi-experiments and true experiments in field settings. In *Handbook of Industrial and Organizational Psychology*, M. Dunnette, (Ed.). pp. 223-324. Chicago: Rand McNally.

Cooke, K. (1982). Guidelines for socially appropriate tourism development in British Columbia. *Journal of Travel Research, 21*, 22-28.

Cooke, O.E. (Ed.). (1970). *Tourism: Passport to Development?* Oxford: Oxford University Press.

Cooper, R. (1977). Images of tourism. *New Society*, 25 August, 385-386.

Couch, A. & Kenniston K. (1960). Yeasayers and naysayers: Agreeing response set as a personality variable, *Journal of Abnormal Social Psychology, 60 (March)*, 171-174.

Countryside Commission. (1979). *Interpretation of Visitor Centres: A Study of the Effectiveness of Interpretive Services*. Cheltenham: Countryside Commission.

Crompton, J.L. (1977). *A System Model of the Tourist's Destination Selection Decision Process with Particular Reference to the Role of Image and Perceived Constraints*. College Station: Texas A and M University, Unpublished Ph.D. Dissertation.

Crompton, J.L. (1979a). An assessment of the image of Mexico as a vacation destination and the influence of geographical location upon that image. *Journal of Travel Research, 17*, 18-23.

Crompton, J.L. (1979b). Motivations for pleasure vacation. *Annals of Tourism Research, 6*, 408-424.

Crompton J.L. (1981). Dimensions of a social group role in pleasure vacations. *Annals of Tourism Research, 8*, 550-568.

Crompton, J.L. & Duray, N.A. (1985). An investigation of the relative efficacy of four alternative approaches to importance-performance analysis. *Journal of the Academy of Marketing Science, 13*, 69-80.

Dann, G. (1977). Anomie, ego-enhancement and tourism. *Annals of Tourism Research, 4*, 184-194.

Dartington Amenity Research Trust. (1974). *Farm Recreation and Tourism in England and Wales.* Dartington: Dartington Amenity Research Trust.

Davis, J. (1967). Clustering and a balance in graphs. *Human Relations, 20*, 181-187.

Day, G.S. & Deutscher, T. (1982). Attitudinal predictions of choices of major appliance brands. *Journal of Marketing Research, 19*, 192-198.

de Kadt, E. (Ed.). (1979). *Tourism: Passport to Development?* Oxford: Oxford University Press.

de Lacey, K. (1987). The dark side of the tourist boom. *The Cairns Post*, 30 October, 6.

Dernoi, L.A. (1983). Farm tourism in Europe. *Tourism Management, 4*, 155-166.

Dougherty, P.H. (1981). New ways to classify consumers. *New York Times*, 25 February.

Downs, R.M. (1970). The cognitive structure of an urban shopping center. *Environment and Behaviour, 2*, 13-39.

Downs, R.M. & Stea, D. (1973). *Image and Environment.* Chicago: Aldine.

Downs, R.M. & Stea, D. (1977). *Maps in Minds: Reflections on Cognitive Mapping.* New York: Harper and Row.

Doxey, G.V. (1975). The causation theory of visitor-resident irritants, methodology, and research inferences. *The Impact of Tourism*, Sixth Annual Conference Proceedings of the Travel Research Association, San Diego, 195-198.

Duffield, B.S. & Long, J. (1982). Tourism in the highlands and islands of Scotland: rewards and conflicts. *Annals of Tourism Research, 8*, 69-90.

Durnoi, L.A. (1983). Farm tourism in Europe. *Tourism Management, 4*, 155-166.

Echtner, C.M. & Brent-Ritchie, J.R. (1991). The meaning and measurement of destination image. *The Journal of Tourism Studies, 2*, 2-12.

Eco, U. (1986). *Travels in Hyper-Reality.* London: Picador.

Eiser, J.R. (1986). *Social Psychology.* Cambridge: Cambridge University Press.

Evans, G.W. (1980). Environmental cognitions. *Psychological Bulletin, 88*, 259-287.

Evans, G.W., Marrero, D.G. & Butler, P.A. (1981). Environmental learning and cognitive mapping. *Environment and Behaviour, 13*, 83-104.

Eysenck, H.J. & Eysenck, S.B. (1970). *The Eysenck Personality Inventory.* San Diego: Edits.

Eysenck, M.A. (1984). *Handbook of Cognitive Psychology.* Hillsdale, N.J.: Laurence Erlbaum.

Farber, M. (1954). Some hypotheses on the psychology of travel. *Psychoanalytic Review, 41*, 267-271.

Farace, R.V., Monge P.R. & Russell H.M. (1977). *Communicating and organizing.* Reading, MA: Addison-Wesley.

Farr, R.M. (1980). Homo socio-psychologicus. In A.J. Chapman and D.M. Jones (Eds). *Models of Man.* Leicester: British Psychological Society.

Farr, R.M. (1984). Social representations: Their role in the design and execution of laboratory experiments. In R.M. Farr and S. Moscovici (Eds).*Social Representations.* Cambridge: Cambridge University Press. pp. 125-148.

Farr, R.M. & Moscovici, S. (Eds). (1984). *Social Representations.* Cambridge: Cambridge University Press.

Farrell, B.H. (1979). Tourism's human conflicts. *Annals of Tourism Research, 6*, 122-136.

Feather, N.T. (1971). Organization and discrepancy in cognitive structures. *Psychological Review, 78*, 355-379.

Feather, N.T. (1975). *Values in Education and Society.* New York: Free Press.

Feather, N.T. (1979a). Value correlates on conservatism. *Journal of Personality and Social Psychology, 37*, 1617-1630.

Feather, N.T. (1979b). Human values and the work situation: Two studies. *Australian Psychologist, 14*, 131-141.

Feather, N.T. (1982a). Human values and the prediction of action: An expectancy-valence analysis. In N.T. Feather (Ed.). *Expectations and Actions: Expectancy-value Models in Psychology.* Hillsdale, N.J.: Erlbaum.

Feather, N.T. (1982b). *Expectations and Actions: Expectancy-valence Models in Psychology.* Hillside, N.J.: Erlbaum.

Feather, N.T. (1988). The meaning and importance of values: Research with the Rokeach Value Survey. *Australian Journal of Psychology, 40,* 377-390.

Feather, N.T., & Barber, J.G. (1983). Depressive reactions and unemployment. *Journal of Abnormal Psychology, 92,* 185-195.

Feather, N.T. & O'Brien, G.E. (1987). Looking for employment: An expectancy-valence analysis of job-seeking behaviour among young people. *British Journal of Psychology, 78,* 251-272.

Feather, N.T. & Peay, E.R. (1975). The structure of terminal and instrumental values: Dimensions and clusters. *Australian Journal of Psychology, 27,* 151-164.

Finney, B.R. & Watson, K.A. (Eds). (1975). *A New Kind of Sugar: Tourism in the Pacific.* Honolulu: East-West Culture Learning Institute.

Fischer, C.S. (1982). *To Dwell Among Friends: Personal Networks in Town and City,* Chicago: University of Chicago Press.

Fischer, C.S. & Phillips S.L. (1979). *Who is Alone? Social Characteristics of People with Small Networks* (Working Paper No. 310). Berkeley: Institute of Urban and Regional Development, University of California.

Fishbein, M. & Ajzen, I. (1975). *Beliefs, Attitude, Intention and Behaviour: An Introduction to Theory and Research.* Reading, MA: Addison-Wesley.

Fiske, D.W. & Maddi, S.R. (1961). *Functions of Varied Experience.* Homewood, IL: Dorsey.

Flanaghan, J.C. (1978). A research approach to improving our quality of life. *American Psychologist, 25,* 138-147.

Forster, J. (1964). The sociological consequences of tourism. *International Journal of Comparative Sociology, 5,* 217-227.

Fottler, M.D. & Bain, T. (1980). Sex differences in occupational aspiration. *Academy of Management Journal, 23,* 144-149.

Fottler, M.D. & Bain, T. (1984). Realism of occupational choice among high school seniors: implications for quality of work life. *Journal of Occupational Behaviour, 5,* 237-251.

Fraisse, P. (1963). *The Psychology of Time.* London: Eyre and Spottiswoode.

Frank, O. (1978). Sampling and estimation in large social networks. *Social Networks, 1,* 91-101.

Frater, J. (1982). Farm tourism in England and overseas. *Birmingham Centre for Urban and Regional Studies, Research Memorandum 93.*

French, J.R.P. & Kahn, R.L. (1962). A programmatic approach to studying the industrial environment and mental health. *Journal of Social Issues, 18,* 1-47.

Frey, R.S. (1984). Need for Achievement, entrepreneurship and economic growth: Critique of the McClelland thesis. *The Social Science Journal, 21,* 125-134.

Furnham, A. (1990). *The Protestant Work Ethic.* London: Routledge.

Furnham, A. & Argyle, M. (Eds). (1981). *The Psychology of Social Situations.* Oxford: Pergamon Press.

Galbraith, J. & Cummings, L.L. (1967). An empirical investigation of the motivational determinants of task performance: Interactive effects between valence-instrumentality and motivation-ability. *Organizational Behaviour and Human Performance, 2,* 237-258.

Galster, G. & Hesser, G. (1981). Residential satisfaction: compositional and contextual correlates. *Environment and Behaviour, 13,* 735-758.

Gartner, W.C. (1986). Temporal influences on image change. *Annals of Tourism Research, 13,* 635-644.

Gartner, W.C. (1989). Tourism image: Attribute measurement of standard tourism products using multidimensional scaling techniques. *Journal of Travel Research, 28,* 15-19.

Gartner, W.C. & Hunt, J.D. (1987). An analysis of state image changeover a twelve year period (1971-1983). *Journal of Travel Research, 16*, 15-19.

Gattas, J., Roberts, K., Reinhard S.S., Water T. & Yvan V. (1986).Leisure and life-styles: Towards a research agenda. *Society and Leisure, 9, (2)* 529-539.

Georgopoulos, B.S., Mahoney, G.M. & Jones, N. (1957). A path-goal approach to productivity. *Journal of Applied Psychology, 41*, 345-353.

Giddens, A. (1976). *New Rules of Sociological Method: A positive Critique of Interpretive Sociologies.* New York: Basic Books.

Gitelson, R.L. & Crompton, J.L. (1983). The planning horizons and sources of information used by pleasure travellers. *Journal of Travel Research, 21*, 2-7.

Gnoth, J. (1997). Tourism motivation and expectation formation. *Annals of Tourism Research, 24*, 283-304.

Goeldner, C. & McIntosh, R. (1984). *Tourism: Principles, Practices and Philosophies.* Columbus, OH: Grid Publishing.

Goldthorpe, J., Lockwood, D., Bechofer, F. & Platt, J. (1968). *The Affluent Worker.* London: Cambridge University Press.

Golledge, R.G. (1978). Learning about urban environments. In T. Carlstein *et al.* (Eds). *Timing Space and Spacing Time.* London: Arnold.

Golledge, R.G. & Rayner, J.N. (1982). *Proximity and Preference: Problems in the Multidimensional Analysis of Large Data Sets.* Minneapolis: University of Minnesota Press.

Goodrich, J.N. (1979). A new approach to image analysis through multidimensional scaling. *Journal of Travel Research, XVI*, 3-7.

Goodrich, J.N. (1978). The relationship between preferences for and perceptions of vacation destinations: Applications of a choice model. *Journal of Travel Research, XVII*, 8-13.

Gould, P. (1963). Man against his environment: A game theoretical framework. *Annals of the Association of American Geographers, 53*, 290-297.

Goudy, W. (1977). Evaluations of local attributes and community satisfaction in small towns. *Rural Sociology, 42*, 371-382.

Graburn, N.H.H. & Jafari, J. (1991). Introduction tourism social science. *Annals of Tourism Research, 18*.

Graen, G. (1969). Instrumentality theory of work motivation: Some experimental results and suggested modifications. *Journal of Applied Psychology, 53*, 2.

Gray, H.P. (1970). *International Travel — International Trade.* Lexington: Heath Lexington Books.

Griffin, R.W., Welsh, A, & Moorehead, G. (1981). Perceived task characteristics and employee performance: A literature review. *Academy of Management Review, 6*, 655-664.

Gunn, C. (1988a). *Vacationscapes: Designing Tourist Regions.* New York: Van Nostrand Reinhold.

Gunn, C.A. (1988b). *Tourism Planning.* New York: Taylor and Francis.

Gurin, G., Veroff, J. & Feld, S., (1960). *Americans View Their Mental Health.* New York: Basic Books.

Gustke, L. (1982). Mental images of the sunbelt as a travel region. PhD. Diss. Texas A and M University, College Station.

Haahti, A. & Yavas, U. (1983). Tourists' perceptions of Finland and selected European countries as travel destinations. *European Journal of Marketing, 12*, 34-42.

Hackman, J.R. & Lawler, E.E. (1971). Employee reactions to job characteristics. *Journal of Applied Psychology, 55*, 259-286.

Hackman, J.R. & Oldham, G.R. (1976). Motivation through the design of work: Test of a theory. *Organisational Behaviour and Human Performance, 16*, 250-279.

Hagerstrand, T. (1952). The propagation of innovation waves. *Studies in Geography, Series B (4).* Lund, Sweden: Gleerup.

Hall, E.T. (1959). *The Silent Language.* New York: Doubleday.

Hall, E.T. (1964). *The Hidden Dimension.* New York: Doubleday.

Hansen, F. (1976). Psychological theories of consumer choice. *Journal of Consumer Research, 3*, 117-142.

Hartman, R. (1988). Combining field methods in tourism research. *Annals of Tourism Research, 15*, 88-105.

Hartshorne, H. & May, M.A. (1930). *Studies in the Nature of Character.* New York: Macmillan.

Hatry, H., Winnie, R. & Fisk, D., (1973). *Practical Program Evaluation for State and Local Government Officials.* Washington, DC: Urban Institute.

Haukeland, J.V. (1990). Sociocultural impacts of tourism in Scandinavia. *Tourism Management, 5*, 207-214.

Hawkins, D.I., Best, R.J. & Coney, K.A.(1983). *Consumer Behaviour: Implications for Marketing Strategy.* Plano, TX: Business Publications.

Haywood, K.M. (1986). Can the tourist area life cycle be made operational? *Tourism Management, September,* 154-167.

Heider, F. (1946). Attitudes and cognitive organization. *Journal of Psychology, 21*, 107-112.

Heider, F. (1958). *The Psychology of Interpersonal Relations.* New York: Wiley.

Heller, K., Price, R.H., Reinharz, S., Rigor, S., Wandersman, A. & D'Aunno, T.A. (1984). *Psychology and Community Change.* Homewood, II: Dorsey Press.

Henshall, B.D. & Roberts, R. (1985). Comparative assessment of tourist generating countries for New Zealand. *Annals of Tourism Research, 12*, 219-238.

Herzberg, F., Mausner, B. & Snyderman, B. (1959). *The Motivation to Work.* New York: Wiley.

Hildebrand, D.K., Laing, J.D. & Rosenthal, H. (1977). *Analysis of Ordinal Data.* Sage University Paper series on Quantitative Applications in the Social Sciences, series No. 07-001. Beverly Hills: Sage Publications.

Hirschman, E.C. & Holbrook, M.B. (1982). Hedonic consumption: Emerging concepts, methods and propositions. *Journal of Marketing, 46*, 92-101.

Ho, R. & Lloyd, J. (1984). Development of an Australian work ethic scale. *Australian Psychologist, 19*, 321-332.

Hoffman, D.L. & Low, S.A. (1978). An application of the probit transformation of tourism survey data. *Journal of Travel Research, 17*, 35-38.

Holdsworth, R. (1982). Organizational Behaviour. In R. Holdsworth (Ed.). *Psychology for Career Counselling.* Leicester: The British Psychological Society.

Homan, R. (1984). A values and life styles perspective on human behaviour. In *Personal Values and Consumer Psychology.* R.E. Pitts & A.G. Woodside, (Eds). Lexington, MA: Lexington Books.

Hooley, G.J., Shipley, D. & Krieger, N. (1988). A method of modelling consumer perceptions of country of origin. *International Marketing Review, Autumn,* 67-76.

Howard, J.A. & Sheth, J.N., (1969). *The Theory of Buyer Behaviour.* New York: Wiley.

Hughes, K. (1991). Tourist satisfaction: A guided 'cultural' tour in North Queensland. *Australian Psychologist, 26*, 166-171.

Hultsman, J. (1995). Just Tourism — An ethical framework. *Annals of Tourism Research, 22*, 553-567.

Hunt, J.D. (1975). Image as a factor in tourism development. *Journal of Travel Research, XIII*, 1.

Inkson, J.H.K. (1971). Achievement motivation and occupational choice. *Australian Journal of Psychology, 23*, 225-234.

Isaac, S., & Michael, W. (1974). *Handbook in Research and Evaluation for Education and the Behavioural Sciences.* San Diego: Robert R. Knapp.

Iso-Ahola, S.E. (1980). *The Social Psychology of Leisure and Recreation.* Dubuque, I.A.: Brown.

Iso-Ahola, S.E. (1982). Toward a social psychological theory of tourism motivation: A rejoinder. *Annals of Tourism Research, 9*, 256-262

Iso-Ahola, S.E. (1983). Toward a social psychology of recreational travel. *Leisure Studies, 2*, 45-56.

Iso-Ahola, S.E. (1984). Social psychological foundations of leisure and resultant implications for leisure counselling. In *Leisure Counselling: Concepts and Applications.* E.T. Dowd (Ed.). Illinois: C.C. Thomas.

Ittelson, W.H. (1973). Environment perceptions and contemporary perceptual theory. In *Environment and Cognition.* W.H. Ittelson. (Ed.). New York: Seminar Press.

Jarratt, P. (1987). Tropical daydream, tropical nightmare. *The Bulletin, March 17th,* 43-48.

Jefferson, A. (1987). Tourism into the 90s. *British Travel Brief, 3,* 10-12.

Jones, L.M. & Fischer C.S. (1978). *Studying Egocentric Networks by Mass Survey* (Working paper no. 284). Berkeley: Institute of Urban and Regional Development, University of California.

Kabanoff, B. & O'Brien, G.E. (1986). Stress and the leisure needs and activities of different occupations. *Human Relations, 39,* 903-916.

Kahle, L.R. (Ed.). (1983). *Social Values and Social Change: Adaptation to Life in America.* New York: Praeger.

Kahle, L.R. (1984a). *Attitudes and Social Adaptation: A Person-Situation Interaction Approach.* Oxford: Pergamon.

Kahle, L.R. (1984b). The values segmentation debate continues. *Marketing News, 18,* 231-237.

Kahle, L.R. (1985). Social values in the eighties: A special issue. *Psychology and Marketing, 2,* 58-65.

Kahle, L.R. (1986). The nine nations of North America and the value basis of geographic segmentation. *Journal of Marketing, 50,* 37-47.

Kahle, L.R, Beatty, S.E. & Homer, P. (1986). Alternative measurement approaches to consumer values. *Journal of Consumer Research, 13,* 405-408.

Kale, S.H. & Weir, K.M. (1986). Marketing third world countries to the western traveller: The case of India. *Journal of Travel Research, 25,* 2-7.

Kaplan, S. & Kaplan, R. (1982). *Cognition and Environment.* New York: Praeger.

Kendall, J.W. & Var, T. (1984). *The Perceived Impact of Tourism: The State of the Art.* Vancouver: Simon Fraser University.

Kennedy, L. (1989). Can you still call Cairns home? *The Cairns Post, January 14th,* 9.

Kent, N. (1977). A new kind of sugar. In R.R. Finney and K.A. Watson (Eds). *A New Kind of Sugar: Tourism in the Pacific.* Santa Cruz, California: Centre for South Pacific Studies, University of California, Santa Cruz, 169-198.

Knebel. H.J. (1960). *Sociologische Strukturwanderlungen im Modernen Tourismus.* Stuttgart: Enke.

Knoke, D. & Kuklinski, J.H. *Network Analysis* (Quantitative Applications in the Social Sciences Series Paper No. 28). Beverly Hills: Sage.

Kotler, P. (1987). Semiotics of person and nation marketing. In J. Umiker-Seboek (Ed.). *Marketing and Semiotics.* Berlin: Mouton de Gruyter.

Kramer, R.M. & Specht, H. (Eds). (1975). *Readings in Community Organization Practice.* Englewood Cliffs, N.J.: Prentice-Hall.

Krippendorf, J. (1987). *The Holiday Makers.* London: Heinemann.

Kruskal, J.B. & Wish M. (1978). *Multidimensional Scaling* (Quantitative Applications in the Social Sciences Series Paper No. 11). Beverly Hills: Sage.

Ladewig, H. & McCann, G.C. (1980). Community satisfaction: theory and measurement. *Rural Sociology, 45,* 110-131.

Lancaster, K.J. (1966). A new approach to consumer theory, *Journal of Political Economy, 74,* 132-157.

Lawler, E.E. (1973). *Motivation in Work Organizations.* Monteray, Calif.: Brooks/Cole.

Lawrence, T.B., Wickins, D. & Phillips, N. (1997). Managing legitimacy in ecotourism. *Tourism Management, 18,* 307-316.

Lawrence, W. & Brown, D. (1976). An investigation of intelligence, self-concept, socio-economic status, race and sex as predictors of career maturity. *Journal of Vocational Behaviour, 9,* 43-52.

Lawson, F. & Baud-Bovy, M. (1977). *Tourism and Recreational Development*. London: Architectural Press.

Lee-Hoxter, A. & Lester, D. (1988). Tourist behaviour and personality, *Personality and Individual Differences, 9,* 177-178.

Leinhardt, S. (1977). Preface. In *Social Networks: A Developing Paradigm,* S. Leinhardt (Ed.). New York: Academic Press.

Leiper, N. (1990). *Tourism Systems.* Occasional Paper No. 2. Auckland: Department   of Management Systems.

Lewin, K. (1951). *Field Theories in Social Science.* New York: Harper.

Lewis E.R. (1977). *Network Models in Population Biology.* New York: Springer-Verlag.

Lewis, R.C. & Pizam, A. (1981). Guest surveys: A missed opportunity. *Cornell Hotel and Restaurant Administration Quarterly, 22,* 37-44.

Lim, S.B. (1988). The boom that's now an explosion. *The Weekend Australian,* 3-4 December, 41-44.

Lindquist, J.D. (1974-75). Meaning of image. *Journal of Retailing, 50,* 30-38.

Litwin, G.H. & Stringer, R.A. (1968). *Motivation and Organisational Climate.* Boston: Division of Research, Graduate School of Business Administration, Harvard University.

Lloyd, R. & Heivly, C. (1987). Systematic distortions in urban cognitive maps. *Annals of the Association of American Geographers, 77,* 191-207.

Loukissas, P. (1983). Public participation in community tourism planning: A gaming stimulation approach. *Journal of Travel Research, 22,* 18-23.

Lowenthal, D. (1972). Research in environmental perception and behaviour: perspectives on current problems. *Environment and Behaviour, 43,* 333-342.

Lowenthal, D. & Prince, H. (1965). English landscape tastes. *Geographical Review, 55,* 186-222.

Lui, J. & Var, T. (1984). *Resident Attitudes to Tourism in Hawaii.* Paper presented at the 15th TTRA Conference, Philadelphia.

Lui, J.C., Sheldon, P.J. & Var, T. (1987). Resident perception of the environmental impacts of tourism. *Annals of Tourism Research, 14,* 17-37.

Lynch, K. (1960). *The Image of the City.* Cambridge, Mass: MIT Press.

MacCannell, D. (1973). Staged authenticity: Arrangements of social space in tourist settings. *American Journal of Sociology, 79,* 589-603.

MacCannell, D. (1976). *The Tourist.* New York: Schocken.

MacFarlane, R.N., (1979). *A Comparative Analysis of Resident-Visitor Contact and Resident Attitudes Toward Tourism.* Paper presented at the Canadian Association of Geographers Annual Meeting, University of Victoria, B.C.

Mackay-Payne, M. (1988). Families despair in a city of plenty. *The Cairns Post,* 6 August, 21.

McClelland, D.C. (1971). *Assessing Human Motivation.* New York: Irvington.

McClelland, D.C. (1985). *The Achieving Society.* New York: Free Press.

McClelland, D.C., Atkinson, J.W., Clark, R.A. & Lowell, E.L. (1953). *The Achievement Motive.* New York: Appleton-Century-Crofts.

Maddox, R.N. (1985). Measuring satisfaction with tourism. *Journal of Travel Research, Winter,* 2-5.

Mann, L. (1977). The effect of stimulus queues on queue joining behaviour. *Journal of Personality and Social Psychology, 35,* 437-442.

Mann, L. & Taylor, K.F. (1969). Queue counting: the effect of motives upon estimates of numbers in waiting lines. *Journal of Personality and Social Psychology, 12,* 95-103.

Mann, P.A. (1978). *Community Psychology Concepts and Applications.* New York: Free Press.

Mannell, R.C. & Iso-Ahola, S.E. (1987). Psychological nature of leisure and tourism experience. *Annals of Tourism Research, 14,* 314-331.

Marsden, P.V. & N. Lin, (Eds). (1982). *Social Structure and Network Analysis.* Beverly Hills: Sage.

Martineau, P. (1957). *Motivation in Advertising.* New York: McGraw-Hill.

Maslow, A.H. (1943). A theory of human motivation. *Psychological Review, 50,* 370-396.

Maslow, A.H. (1954). *Motivation and Personality.* NY: Harper & Brothers.

Maslow, A.H. (1965). *Eupsychian Management.* Homewood, Ill.: Irwin.

Maslow, A.H. (1970). *Motivation and Personality.* New York: Harper & Row.

Matejka, J.K. (1973). Critical factors in vacation area selection. *Arkansas Business and Economic Review, 6,* 17-19.

Matheson, A. and Wall, G. (1982). *Tourism: Economic, Physical and Social Impacts.* New York: Wiley.

Maude, A.J.S. & van Rest, D.J. (1985). The social and economic effects of farm tourism in the United Kingdom. *Agricultural Administration, 20,* 85-98.

Mayo, E. (1975). Tourism and the national parks: A psychographic and attitudinal study. *Journal of Travel Research, 14,* 14-18.

Mayo, E. & Jarvis, L.P. (1981). *The Psychology of Leisure Travel.* Boston: CBI Publishing.

Mayo, E.J. (1973). Regional images and regional travel destination. *In Proceedings of The Fourth Annual Conference of TTRA.* pp. 211-217. Salt Lake City UT: Travel and Tourism Research Association.

McIntosh, R.W. (1977). *Tourism — Principles, Practices, Philosophies.* NY: Wiley.

McKay, K.J. & Fesenmaier, D.R. (1997). Pictorial elements of destination image formation. *Annals of Tourism Research, 24,* 537-565.

Mehrabian, A. (1972). *Nonverbal Communication.* Chicago: Aldine Atherton.

Mehrabian, A. & Russell, J.A. (1974). *An Approach to Environmental Psychology.* Cambridge, MA: M.I.T. Press.

Melton, A.W. (1972). Visitor behaviour in museums: Some early research in environmental design. *Human Factors, 14,* 393-403.

Meulemann, H. (1987). From life chances to life style: On some effects of educational expansion on the change of achievement values. *Social Science Information, 26, (3),* 513-33.

Meyersohn, R. (1981). *Tourism as a Socio-Cultural Phenomenon: Research Perspectives.* Research Paper No 3 of the Research Group on Leisure and Cultural Development. Waterloo: Otium Publications.

Middelstaedt, R.A., Grossbart, S.L. & Curtin, W.W. (1977). Consumer perceptions and retail mapping: Research findings and preliminary theory. In *Consumer and Industrial Buying Behaviour,* A.G. Woodside, A.G.S. Jagdish & P.D. Bennett (Eds). New York: North-Holland.

Milgram, S. (1967). The small world problem. *Psychology Today, 1,* 61-67.

Mill, R.C. & Morrison, A.M. (1985). *The Tourism System.* Englewood Cliffs, NJ: Prentice-Hall.

Milman, A. and Pizam A. (1995). The role of awareness and familiarity with a destination: The Central Florida case. *Journal of Travel Research.*

Min Han, C. (1989). Country image: Halo or summary construct? *Journal of Marketing Research, XXVII,* 222-229.

Mitchell, A. (1983). *The Nine American Life Styles.* New York: Warner.

Mitchell, J.C. (1969). The concept and use of social networks. In *Social networks in urban situations.* J.C. Mitchell (Ed.). Manchester: Manchester University Press.

Mitchell, J.R., Dowling, P.J., Kabanoff, B.V. & Larson, J.R. (1988). *People in Organizations.* Sydney: McGraw-Hill.

Moreno, J.L. (1951). *Sociometry, Experimental Method, and the Science of Society.* New York: Beacon House.

Morley, C.L. (1990). What is tourism? *The Journal of Tourism Studies, 1,* 3-8.

Morrison, J.K. (Ed.). (1979). *A Consumer Approach to Community Psychology.* Chicago: Nelson-Hall.

Morse, N.C. & Weiss, R.S. (1955). The function and meaning of work and job. *American Sociological Review, 20,* 191-198.

Moscardo, G. (1988). Toward a cognitive model of visitor responses in interpretive centres. *Journal of Environmental Education, 20,* 29-38.

Moscardo, G. (1991). Museum Scripts: An example of the application of social cognitive research to tourism. *Australian Psychologist, 26,* 158-165.

Moscardo, G. & Pearce, P.L. (1986). Visitor centres and environmental interpretation: An exploration of the relationships among visitor enjoyment, understanding and mindfulness. *Journal of Environmental Psychology, 6,* 89-108.

Moscovici, S. (1973). Forward. In C. Herzlich. *Health and Illness.* London: Academic Press.

Moscovici, S. (1976). *Social Influence and Social Change.* London: Academic Press.

Mukerji, C. (1978). Bullshitting: Road lore among hitchhikers. *Social Problems, 25,* 241-252.

Munson, J. M. (1984). Personal values: Considerations on their measurement and application of five areas of research inquiry. In *Personal Values and Consumer Psychology,* R.E. Pitts Jr. & A.G. Woodside, (Eds). Lexington, MA: Lexington Books.

Murdoch, S.H. & Shriner, E.C. (1979). Community service satisfaction and states community development: An examination of evidence from impacted communities. *Journal of Community Development Society, 10,* 109-123.

Murphy, H.P. & Hodel, G. H. (1980). *INTRAMAR — East: A Study of Some of the World's Great Airlines, Hotels, and Destinations.* Manila: International Travel Research Institute International Research Associates (Asia) Ltd.

Murphy, P.E. (1980). Perceptions and preferences of decision-making groups in tourist centers: a guide to planning strategy? In D.E. Hawkins, E.L. Shafer & J.M. Rovelstad (Eds). *Tourism Planning and Development Issues,* Washington, D.C.: George Washington University Press, 355-367.

Murphy, P.E. (1981). Community attitudes to tourism: A comparative analysis. *International Journal of Tourism Management, 2,* 189-195.

Murphy, P.E. (1983). Perceptions and attitudes of decision-making groups in tourism centers. *Journal of Travel Research, XXI,* 8-12.

Murphy, P.E. (1985). *Tourism: A Community Approach.* New York: Methuen.

Murray, H.A. (1938). *Explorations in Personality.* New York: Oxford University Press.

Myer, D.G. (1986). *Psychology.* New York: Worth.

Nickerson, N.P. & Ellis, G.D. (1991). Traveller type and activation theory: A comparison of two models, *Journal of Travel Research, XXIX,* 26-31.

Nielson, R.A. (1989). Mudflats vital (Letter to the editor). *The Cairns Post,* 21 February, 7.

Nolan, S.D. (1976). Tourists use and evaluation of travel information sources: Summary and conclusions. *Journal of Travel Research, 14,* 6-8.

O'Brien, G.E. (1982). Evaluation of the job characteristics theory of work attitudes and performance. *Australian Journal of Psychology, 34,* 383-401.

O'Brien, G.E. (1983). Locus of control, work, and retirement. In H.M. Lefcourt (Ed.). *Research in Locus of Control.* Vol 3. New York: Academic Press, 7-21.

Oeser, O.A. & O'Brien, G.E. (1967). A mathematical model for structural role theory. *Human Relations, III,* 83-97.

Osgood, C.E., Suci, G.J. & Tannenbaum, P.H. (1957). *The Measurement of Meaning.* Urbana, Illinois: University of Illinois Press.

Park, C.W. (1978). A conflict resolution choice model. *Journal of Consumer Research, 5,* 124-137.

Park C.W. & Luts, R.J. (1982). Decision plans and consumer choice dynamics. *Journal of Marketing Research, 19,* 108-115.

Parsons, P. & Loomis, R.J. (1973). *Patterns of Museum Visitor Exploration: Then and Now.* Washington, D.C: Smithsonian Institute.

Pearce, D.G. (1981). A systematic comparison of travel-related roles. *Human Relations, 38,* 1001-1011.

Pearce, P.L. (1977). Mental souvenirs: A study of tourists and their city maps. *Australian Journal of Psychology, 29,* 203-210.

Pearce, P.L. (1981). Route maps: A study of travellers' perceptions of a section of country-side. *Journal of Environmental Psychology, 1*, 141-155.

Pearce, P.L. (1982a). Perceived changes in holiday destinations. *Annals of Tourism Research, 9*, 145-164.

Pearce, P.L. (1982b). *The Social Psychology of Tourist Behaviour.* Oxford: Pergamon.

Pearce, P.L. (1984). Tourist-guide interaction. *Annals of Tourism Research, 11*, 129-146.

Pearce P.L. (1988). *The Ulysses Factor: Evaluating Visitors in Tourist Settings.* New York: Springer-Verlag.

Pearce, P.L. (1989). Towards the better management of tourist queues. *Tourism Management, Dec*, 279-284.

Pearce, P.L. (1990a). Personal communication.

Pearce, P.L. (1990c). *The Backpacker Phenomenon.* Townsville: The James Cook University of North Queensland.

Pearce, P.L. (1990d). Farm tourism in New Zealand: A social situation analysis. *Annals of Tourism Research, 17*, 337-352.

Pearce, P.L. & Caltabiano, M.L. (1983). Inferring travel motivation from travellers' experiences, *Journal of Travel Research, XXII*, 16-20.

Pearce, P.L. & Moscardo, G. (1984). Making sense of tourists' complaints. *International Journal of Tourist Management, 5*, 20-23.

Pearce, P.L. & Moscardo, G. (1985). Visitor evaluation: An appraisal of goals and techniques. *Evaluation Review, 9*, 281-306.

Pearce, P.L. & Moscardo, G.M. (1986). The concept of authenticity in tourist experiences. *Australian and New Zealand Journal of Sociology, 22*, 121-132.

Pearce, P.L. Moscardo, G.M. & Ross G.F. (1991). Tourism impact and community perception: An equity/social representational perspective. *Australian Psychologist, 26*, 147-152.

Pearce, P.L. & Stringer, P.F. (1991). Psychology and tourism. *Annals of Tourism Research, 18*, 136-154.

Phelps, A. (1986). Holiday destination image — The problem of assessment: An example developed in Menorca. *Tourism Management, September*, 168-180.

Pigram, J.J. (1980). Environmental implications of tourism development. *Annals of Tourism Research, VII*, 554-583.

Pi-Sunyer, O. (1978). Through native eyes: Tourists and tourism in a Catalan maritime community. In V. Smith (Ed.). *Hosts and Guests.* Oxford: Blackwell.

Pizam, A. (1978). Tourism's impacts: The social costs to the destination community as perceived by its residents. *Journal of Travel Research, XVI*, 8-12.

Pizam, A. (1980). Evaluating social impacts of tourism: The case of Cape Cod, Massachusetts. *Tourism Recreation Research, December*, 3-7.

Pizam, A. (1982). Tourism and crime: Is there a relationship? *Journal of Travel Research, XX*, 7-10.

Plog, S.C. (1968). *New Markets for Air Travel: Executive Summary.* Vol 1. Panorama City, CA: Behavioural Science Corporation.

Plog, S.C. (1972). *Why Destination Areas Rise and Fall in Popularity.* Paper presented to the Travel Research Association Southern California Chapter, Los Angeles, October.

Plog, S.C. (1973). Why destination areas rise and fall in popularity. *Cornell Hotel and Restaurant Administration Quarterly, 15*, 55-59.

Plog, S.C. (1979). *Where in the World are People Going and Why do They Want to go There?* Paper presented to Tianguis Turistico, Mexico City, Mexico.

Plog, S. (1987). The uses and demands for psychographic research. In J.R. Brent-Richie & C.R. Goeldner (Eds). *Travel, Tourism and Hospitality Research.* New York: J. Wiley and Sons.

Porter, L.W. & Lawler, E.E. (1968). *Managerial Attitudes and Performance.* Homewood Il.: Irwin.

Price, F.V. (1981). Only connect? Issues in charting social networks. *Sociological Review, 29*, 283-312.

Pritchard, R.D. & Karasik, B.W. (1973). The effects of organisational climate on managerial job performance and satisfaction. *Organisational Behaviour and Human Performance, 13*, 392-403.

Pryor, P.T.I. (1980). An assessment of residents' attitudes and tourism employment in the Cook Islands. In D. Pearce (Ed.). *Tourism in the South Pacific.*

Przeclawski, K. (1985). The role of tourism in contemporary culture. *The Tourist Review, 40*, 2-6.

Rajotte, F. (1977). Evaluating the cultural and environmental impact of Pacific tourism. *Pacific Perspective, 6*, 41-48.

Reason, J. (1964). *Man in Motion: The Psychology of Travel.* New York: Walker.

Reilly, M.D. (1990). Free elicitation of descriptive adjectives for tourism image assessment. *Journal of Travel Research, 28*, 21-26.

Reynolds, H.T. (1977). *Analysis of Nomina Data.* Sage University paper series on Quantitative Applications in the Social Sciences, series No. 07-001. Beverley Hills: Sage Publications.

Reynolds, T. J. & Jolly J.P. (1980). Measuring personal values: An evaluation of alternative methods. *Journal of Marketing Research, 17*, 531-536.

Reynolds, W.H. (1965). The role of the consumer in image building. *California Management Review, Spring*, 69-76.

Richardson, S.L. & Crompton, J.L. (1988). Cultural variations in perceptions of vacation attributes. *Tourism Management, June*, 128-136.

Riesman, D., Glazer, N. & Denney, R. (1950). *The Lonely Crowd.* New Haven, CT: Yale University Press.

Riley, R.W. (1995). Prestige-worthy tourism behaviour. *Annals of Tourism Research, 22*, 630-649.

Riley, P.J. (1988). Road culture of international long-term budget travellers. *Annals of Tourism Research, 15*, 313-328.

Ritchie, J.R.B. & Goeldner C.R., (Eds). (1987). *Travel, Tourism and Hospitality Research.* New York: Wiley.

Rivers, P. (1973). Tourist troubles. *New Society*, 1 February, 250.

Robinson, E.S. (1928). *The Behaviour of the Museum Visitor.* Washington, D.C.: American Association of Museums.

Roethlisberger, F.J. & Dickson, W.J. (1939). *Management and the Worker.* Cambridge, Mass: Harvard University Press.

Rogers, E.M. (1987). Progress, problems and prospects for network research: Investigating relationships in the age of electronic communication technologies. *Social Networks, 9*, 285-310.

Rogers, E.M. & Kincaid, D.L. (1981). *Communication Networks: Toward a New Paradigm for Research.* New York: Free Press.

Rokeach, M. (1973). *The Nature of Human Values.* New York: Free Press.

Rokeach, M. & Kliejunas, P. (1972). Behaviour as a function of attitude-toward-object and attitude-toward-situation. *Journal of Personality and Social Psychology, 22*, 194-201.

Rosenberg, M.J. (1956). Cognitive structure and attitudinal effect. *Journal of Abnormal and Social Psychology, 53*, 367-372.

Ross, G.F. (1985). *The pathway to court: some community psychology perspectives on predispositions to matrimonial litigiousness.* Unpublished doctoral dissertation, James Cook University of North Queensland, Townsville.

Ross, G.F. (1987). *Some conceptual and methodological issues and procedures related to evaluation of tourist behaviour within the context of an historical display.* Unpublished manuscript, Darwin Institute of Technology.

Ross, G.F. (1988). Destination attraction and Kakadu: Factors associated with the touristic attractiveness of Kakadu National Park. In B. Faulkner and M. Fagence (Eds.). *Frontiers in Australian Tourism.* pp. 317-328. Canberra: Bureau of Tourism Research.

Ross, G.F. (1989a). *Tourism and the City of Cairns: Responses of the Residents.* Paper presented at the Conference of the Royal Australian Planning Institute (Qld Division)/Local Government Planners' Association, Cairns.

Ross, G.F. (1989b). Touristic evaluation within the context of an historic gaol. *Australian Evaluation Society Bulletin, 4,* 18-22.

Ross, G.F. (1990a). Evaluation of touristic contexts: The usefulness of some theoretical formulations. *Proceedings of the 1990 Australian Evaluation Society National Conference, 2,* 81-86.

Ross, G.F. (1990b). Resident responses to the impacts of tourist development. *People and Physical Environment Research, 33,* 2-16.

Ross, G.F. (1990c). *Tourism Impact Judgements: A Study in the Cairns Community.* Paper presented at the Annual Australian Psychological Society conference, University of Melbourne/Monash University, September 1990.

Ross, G.F. (1991a). Tourist destination images of the wet tropical rainforests of North Queensland. *Australian Psychologist, 26,* 147-153.

Ross, G.F. (1991b). The impact of tourism on regional Australian communities. *Regional Journal of Social Issues, 25,* 15-21.

Ross, G.F. (1991c). Correlates of work responses in the tourist industry. *Psychological Reports, 68,* 1079-1083.

Ross, G.F. (1991d). School leavers and their perceptions of employment in the tourism/hospitality industry. *Journal of Tourism Research, 2,* 28-35.

Ross, G.F. (1992a). Resident perceptions of the impact of tourism on an Australian city. *Journal of Travel Research, XXX,* 13-17.

Ross, G.F. (1992b). Tourist motivation among backpacker visitors to the Wet Tropics of Northern Australia. *Journal of Travel and Tourism, 1,* 43-59.

Ross, G.F. (1993). Destination evaluations and vacation preferences among budget travellers. *Annals of Tourism Research, 20,* 477-489.

Ross, G.F. (1994). *The Psychology of Tourism.* Melbourne: Hospitality Press.

Rothman, R.A. (1978). Residents and transients: Community reaction to seasonal visitors. *Journal of Travel Research, XVI,* 8-13.

Rotter, J.B. (1966). Generalized expectancies for internal versus external control of reinforcement. *Psychological Monographs, 80,* No 1.(Whole No. 609).

Ryan, C. and Dewar, K. (1995). Evaluating the communication process between interpreter and visitor. *Tourism Management, 16,* 295-303.

Saarinen, T.F. (1973). Student views of the world. In R.M. Downs and D. Stea, (Eds). *Image and Environment.* Chicago: Aldine.

Sandy, F.A. (1983). *Visitor Industry Report: North West Region of Victoria. Volume 2. Host Community Attitudes to the Visitors.* Melbourne: Footscray Institute of Technology.

Schank, R.C. & Abelson, R.C. (1977). *Scripts, Plans, Goals and Understanding.* Hillsdale, NJ: Lawrence Erlbaum.

Schmidhauser, H. (1989). Tourist needs and motivations. In *Tourism Marketing and Management Handbook.* S.F. Witt and L. Moutinho, (Eds). Hemel Hempstead: Prentice Hall.

Shouten, F. (1995). Improving visitor care in heritage attractions. *Tourism Management, 16,* 259-261.

Schreyer, R. & Lime D.W. (1984). A novice isn't necessarily a novice: The influence of experience use history on subjective perceptions of recreation participation. *Leisure Sciences, 6,* 131-149.

Schultz, D. (1981). *Theories of Personality.* Belmont, Calif.: Wadsworth.

Scott, D., Schewe, C.D. & Frederick, D.G. (1978). A multi-brand/multi-attribute model of tourist state choice. *Journal of Travel Research, 17,* 23-29.

Settle, R., Alreck, P. & Belch M. (1978). Social class determinants of leisure activity. *Advances in Consumer Research, 6,* 139-145.

Sheldon, P. & Var, T. (1984). Resident attitudes to tourism in North Wales. *Tourism Management, 5,* 40-48.

Sheth, J.N. (1974). A field study of attitude structure and the attitude behaviour relationship. In J. Sheth. (Ed.). *Models of Buyer Behaviour.* 242-268. New York: Harper and Row.

Smith, V.L. (Ed.). (1977). *Hosts and Guests: The Anthropology of Tourism.* Philadelphia: University of Pennsylvania Press.

Smith, V.L. (1980). Anthropology and tourism: A science-industry evaluation. *Annals of Tourism Research, 7,* 13-33.

Sommer, R. (1978). *The Mind's Eye: Imagery in Everyday Life.* New York: Dell.

South Australian Division of Tourism. (1976). *The Impact of Tourism on Hahndorf.* Adelaide: The South Australian Department of Tourism, Recreation and Sport.

Spector, P.E. (1982). Behaviour in organizations as a function of employee's locus of control. *Psychological Bulletin, 91,* 482-497.

Spector, P.E. (1985). Higher-order need strength as a moderator of the job scope-employee outcome relationships: A meta-analysis. *Journal of Occupational Psychology, 58,* 119-127.

Spector, P.E. (1988). Development of work locus of control scale. *Journal of Occupational Psychology, 61,* 335-340.

Stagner, R. (1950). Psychological aspects of industrial conflict: II Motivation. *Personnel Psychology, 3,* 1-16.

Steers, R.M. & Braunstein, D.N. (1976). A behaviourally-based measure of manifest needs in work settings. *Journal of Vocational Behaviour, 9,* 251-266.

Stowkowski, P.A. (1990). Extending the social groups model: Social network analysis in recreation research. *Leisure Sciences, 12,* 251-263.

Stringer, P. (1981). Hosts and Guests: The bed-and-breakfast phenomenon. *Annals of Tourism Research, 8,* 357-376.

Stringer, P.F. & Pearce, P.L. (1984). Toward a symbiosis of social psychology and tourism studies. *Annals of Tourism Research, 11,* 5-17.

The Department for Economic and Social Information and Policy analysis of the United Nations (1992). *Statistical Yearbook.* New York: United Nations.

Tichy, N.M., Tushman, M.L. & Fombrun, C. (1979). Social network analysis for organizations. *Academy of Management Review 4,* 507-519.

Tilden, F. (1957). *Interpreting Our Heritage.* Chapel Hill, NC: University of North Carolina Press.

Thomason, P., Crompton, J.L. & Kamp, B.D. (1979). A study of the attitudes of impacted groups within a host community toward prolonged stay tourist visitors. *Journal of Travel Research, XVII,* 2-7.

Thompson, J.R. & Cooper, P.D. (1979). Attitudinal evidence on the limited size of evoked set of travel destinations. *Journal of Travel Research, 17,* 23-25.

Thornton, P.R., Shaw, G. & Williams, A.M. (1997). Tourism group holiday decision-making and behaviour: the influence of children. *Tourism Management, 18,* 287-297.

Thrane, C. (1997). Values as segmentation criteria in tourism research: The Norwegian Monitor approach. *Tourism Management, 18,* 111-113.

Toffler, A. (1970). *Future Shock.* New York: Random House.

Tourism Canada. (1987). *Pleasure Travel Markets to North America: United Kingdom.* Toronto: Market Facts of Canada.

Tourism Training Queensland. (1990). *Think Tourism, Think Careers.* Brisbane: The Queensland Tourism and Hospitality Industry Training Council.

Travers, J. & Milgram S. (1969). An experimental study of the small world problem. *Sociometry, 32,* 425-443.

Travis, A.S. (1982). Managing the environment and cultural impacts of tourism and leisure development. *Tourism Management, 3,* 256-262.

Tribe, J. (1997). The indiscipline of tourism. *Annals of Tourism Research, 24,* 638-657.

Tuan, Y. (1974). *Topophilia.* Englewood Cliffs, N.J.: Prentice-Hall.

Tybout, A.M. & Hauser, J.R. (1981). A marketing audit using a conceptual model of consumer behaviour: Application and evaluation. *Journal of Marketing, 45,* 82-101.

Tysoe, M. (1985). Tourism is good for you. *New Society,* 16 August, 226-230.

Um, S. & Crompton, J.L. (1978). Measuring resident's attachment levels in a host community. *Journal of Travel Research, Summer*, 27-28.

Um, S. & Crompton, J.L. (1990). Attitude determinants in tourism destination choice. *Annals of Tourism Research, 17*, 432-448.

Um, S. & Crompton, J. L. (1991). Development of pleasure travel attitude dimensions. *Annals of Tourism Research, 18*, 374-378.

UNESCO, (1966). *Resolution on the Preservation and Presentation of the Cultural Heritage in Connection with the Promotion of Tourism*. Paris: UNESCO.

Van Raaij, W.F. & Francken D.A. (1984). Vacation decisions, activities and satisfactions. *Annals of Tourism Research, 11*, 101-112.

Var, T., Beck, R.A.D. & Loftus, P. (1977). Determinants of touristic attractiveness of the touristic areas in British Columbia. *Journal of Travel Research, 15*, 23-29.

Var, T., Kendall, K.W. & Tarakcioglu, E. (1985). Resident attitudes toward tourists in a Turkish resort town. *Annals of Tourism Research, 12*, 652-658.

Veltri, J. J. & Schiffman, L.G. (1984). Fifteen years of consumer lifestyle and value research at AT and T. In *Personal Values and Consumer Psychology*. R.E. Pitts &. A.G. Woodwise, (Eds.). Lexington, MA: Lexington Books.

Veroff, J., Douvan, E. & Kulka, R.A. (1981). *The Inner American*. New York: Basic Books.

Vinson, D.E., Scott, J.E. & Lamont, L.M. (1977). The role of personal values in marketing and consumer behaviour. *Journal of Marketing, 41*, 44-50.

von Bertalanffy, L. (1950). The theory of open systems in physics and biology. *Science, 111*, 23-28.

Vogeler, I. (1977). Farm and ranch vacationing. *Journal of Leisure Research, 9*, 271-300.

Vroom, V.H. (1959). Some personality determinants of the effects of participation. *Journal of Abnormal and Social Psychology, 59*, 322-327.

Vroom, V.H. (1964). *Work and Motivation*. New York: Wiley.

Vroom, V.H. & Deci, E.L. (1978). *Management and Motivation*. Harmondsworth: Penguin.

Wahba, M.A. & Bridwell, L.G. (1976). Maslow reconsidered: A review of research on the need hierarchy theory. *Organizational Behaviour and Human Performance, 15*, 212-240.

Walmsley, D.J., Boskovic, R.M. & Pigram, J.J. (1983). Tourism and crime: An Australian perspective. *Journal of Leisure Research, 15*, 136-155.

Walmsley, D.J. & Jenkins, J.M. (1992). Mental maps, Locus of Control and activity: A study of business tourism in Coffs Harbour. *Journal of Tourism Studies, 2*, 36-42.

Walter, C.K. & Hsin-Min, Tong. (1977). A local study of consumer vacation decisions. *Journal of Travel Research, 15*, 30-34.

Wanhill, S.R.C. (1980). Charging for congestion at tourist attractions. *International Journal of Tourism Management, 1*, 168-174.

Washbourne, R.F. & Wagar, J.A. (1972). Evaluating visitor response to exhibit content. *Curator, 15*, 248-254.

Wearing, R.J. (1979). *The impact of tourism on Phillip Island*. Unpublished manuscript, La Trobe University.

Wearing, R.J. (1981). *Tourism: Blessing for Bright*. Canberra: Australian Institute of Urban Studies.

Wellman, B. (1979). The community question: The intimate networks of East Yorkers. *American Journal of Sociology, 84*, 1201-1231.

Wellman, B. (1988). Structural analysis: From method and metaphor to theory and substance. In *Social Structures: A Network Approach*. B. Wellman and S.D. Berkowitz (Eds.). Cambridge: Cambridge University Press.

Wellman, B & Berkowitz, (Eds.) (1998a). *Social structures: A network approach*. Cambridge: Cambridge University Press.

Wellman, B. & Berkowitz, S.D. (Eds.) (1988b). Introduction: Studying social structures. In *Social structures: A network approach*, B. Wellman & S.D. Berkowitz (Eds.). Cambridge: Cambridge University Press.

Wells, W.D. (1966). General personality tests and consumer behaviour. In *On Knowing the Consumer*. J.W. Newman, (Ed.). New York: John Wiley & Sons, pp. 187-189.

Wells, W.D. (1974). *Life Style and Psychographics*, Chicago: American Marketing Association.

Wells, W.D. (1975). Psychographics: A critical review. *Journal of Market Research, 12* (May), 196-312.

Wells, W.D. & Beard A.D. (1973). Personality and consumer behaviour. In *Consumer Behaviour: Theoretical Sources*, S. Ward and T.S. Robertson, (Eds.). Englewood Cliffs, N.J.: Prentice-Hall, pp. 141-199.

West, P.C. (1982). A nationwide test of the status group dynamics approach to outdoor recreation demand. *Leisure Sciences 5*, 1-18.

White, G., Kates R. & Burton, I. (1963). *The Environment as Hazard.* New York: Oxford University Press.

White H.C., Boorman, S.A. & Breiger R.C. (1976). Social structure from multiple networks 1: Block models of roles and positions. *American Journal of Sociology, 81*, 730-780.

White, J.K. (1978). Individual differences and the job quality-worker response relations: Review integration and comments. *Academy of Management Review, 3*, 267-280.

Williams, D.R., Ellis, G.D. & Daniels, C. (1986). *An Empirical Examination of Travel Personality and Travel Destination Preferences.* Paper presented to the National Recreation and Parks Association Conference, Anaheim, CA.

Wohlwill, J.F. (1966). The physical environment: A problem for a psychology of stimulation. *Journal of Social Issues, 12*, 29-38.

Wolff, K.A. trans ed. (1950). *The Sociology of Georg Simmel.* New York: Free Press.

Wolpert, J. (1964). The decision process in a spatial context. *Annals of the Association of American Geographers, 54*, 537-558.

Wolpert, J. (1966). Migration as an adjustment to environmental stress. *Journal of Social Issues, 22*, 92-102.

Woods, W.A. (1981). *Consumer Behaviour.* New York: North-Holland.

Woodside, A.G. & Lysonski, S. (1989). A general model of traveller destination choice. *Journal of Travel Research, 27*, 8-14.

Woodside, A.G. & Ronkainen, I.A. (1980). Tourist management strategies for competitive vacation destinations. In *Tourism Marketing and Management Issues*. D.E. Hawkins, E.C. Shafer & J.M. Rovelstad. (Eds.).Washington DC: George Washington University Press.

Woodside, A.G. Ronkainen, I.A. & Reid D.M. (1977). Measurement and utilization of the evoked sets as a travel marketing variable. In *Proceedings of Eighth Annual Conference of TTRA*, 123-130. Salt Lake City UT: Travel and Tourism Research Association.

Woodside, A.G. & Sherrell, D. (1977). Traveller evoked set, inept set, and inert sets of vacation destinations. *Journal of Travel Research, 16*, 14-18.

World Tourism Organization. (1980). *Tourist Images.* Madrid: WTO.

World Tourism Organization. (1986). *Yearbook of Tourism Statistics.* Madrid: WTO.

Yankelovich, D. (1964). New criteria for market segmentation. *Harvard Business Review (March/April)*, 83-90.

Young, G. (1973). *Tourism: Blessing or Blight?* Harmondsworth: Penguin.

Yuspeh, S. (1984). Syndicated values/life styles segmentation schemes: Use them as descriptive tools, not to select targets. *Marketing News, 18*, 12.

Zimmer, Z., Blayley, R.E. and Searle, M.S. (1995). Whether to go and where: Identification of Important influences on seniors' decisions to travel. *Journal of Travel Research*, Winter, 3-10.

Zube, H. (1976). Perceptions of landscape and land use. In I. Altman and J.F. Wohlwill (Eds). *Human Behaviour and Environment: Advances in Theory and Research, Vol. 1.* 87-121. New York: Plenum.

Index